Little Crowns and How to Win them

Joseph A Collier, Joseph A Collier

BIBLIOLIFE

𝕷𝖎𝖙𝖙𝖑𝖊 𝕮𝖗𝖔𝖜𝖓𝖘

AND

HOW TO WIN THEM.

BY

REV. JOSEPH A. COLLIER,
KINGSTON, N. Y.

NEW·YORK:
ROBERT CARTER & BROTHERS,
No. 580 BROADWAY.
1863.

EDWARD O. JENKINS,
Printer & Stereotyper,
No 20 North William St.

CONTENTS.

—❖—

INTRODUCTION.

———✥———

"Mamma," said a little girl to her mother, one Sabbath, when she had come home from church, "Why don't the minister sometimes preach so that little children like me can understand him?" A few moments afterwards she was seen with her bonnet on, running out of the door. "Where are you going, my dear?" "I am going over to the minister's," said she, "to ask him if he won't please to *preach small.*"

Now, this is just what all the children want, not "small talk," but that we should "talk small" to them. And this is what the writer of these short sermons has tried to do in the children's services which are held regularly in his own church. The thought that he might, in this book, preach them to a still larger congregation, leads him to print them.

May the Good Shepherd bless this tender food to His own dear lambs, for Christ's sake, Amen!

I.

The Child-King.

" THESE are the crowns that we shall wear,
   When all Thy saints are crowned;
These are the palms that we shall bear
   On yonder holy ground.

" Then welcome toil, and care, and pain !
   And welcome sorrow, too !
All toil is rest, all grief is gain,
   With such a prize in view.

" Come, crown and throne ! come, robe and palm !
   Burst forth glad stream of peace !
Come, holy city of the Lamb !
   Rise, Sun of Righteousness !"

The Child-King.

"Josiah was eight years old when he began to reign."—
2 Chronicles xxxiv. 1.

WHAT boy has not sometimes wished that he might become a *king*, and live in a splendid palace, all shining with gold and gems? What girl has not thought how grand it would be to sit on the throne of a *queen*, with her satin and diamonds, and glorious crown, which, like the wishing-cap of the old fairy-tale, would be the means of fulfilling all her desires? Now, I am going to tell you, before I get through, how you may *all wear crowns*, if you will only take the pains to win them.

But I wish now to tell you a true story about a child who was king in Jerusalem, and who sat on a golden throne and wore

(9)

a golden crown, when he was only *eight
years old.* His name was Josiah. His
father, Amon, was a very wicked man ; and
as the Bible says that " the wicked shall not
live out half his days," so Amon was killed
when he was but twenty-four years old.
Then the people put the crown upon the
head of his little son, and made him their
king. He lived in the beautiful palace, and
had a great many servants, horses and
chariots, and everything else that this
world can give to make a child or a man
happy.

But the best of all was this : he had *two
crowns.* The people gave him one, and
God gave him the other. The one was
bright and dazzling as it rested upon his
little head ; the other, more grand and
glorious, he wore upon his heart. The one
was seen and admired by men : the other,
unseen by men, was yet more beautiful to
the eyes of God and the holy angels. What

was this *other* crown? It was *piety*—goodness of heart, love to God and to man. Without this, all the crowns and kingdoms in the world could not have made him happy. With this, he would have been every inch a king, even though he had walked the streets of Jerusalem in the rags of a beggar.

How did he get this other and better crown? One would suppose that the son of wicked Amon would not have been a very good boy; for bad fathers are apt to have worse children. But Josiah had a pious grandfather, whose name was Manasseh, who had died only two years before. No doubt he had often taken the dear child upon his knee, and told him about good king David, and about God and heaven. It is a sad thing to have a wicked parent; but it is a blessed thing to have a grandfather or grandmother who loves the Saviour, and tries to lead little feet to thrones and crowns

in glory. Josiah did not forget the sweet
lessons he had been taught, but "while he
was yet young," as the Bible tells us, "he
began to seek after the God of David, his
father." He sought Him "*early*," and he
sought Him *earnestly*, and we know—for
God has said so—that they who seek Him
early *shall find Him*. So the little king
found God, and when he found Him, he
found his brightest crown. For we read
that "he did that which was right in the
sight of the Lord:" that, like a good missionary, he broke ·down the altars and
images of the heathen idols, which the
people worshipped; that he had God's
beautiful house, which was fast going to
ruin, put in good order; and that he had the
people taught out of the Bible, and did all
that he could by his prayers, his tears, and
his labors, to make every one around him
love and serve the true God.

What a noble life a man can lead who

begins to seek after God when he is a child! But at last, like all other kings, Josiah died. He could no longer wear the earthly crown. But his other crown grew brighter and brighter, and he has been wearing it ever since in heaven, and he will always wear it, for it has become "a crown of glory that fadeth not away."

I have said that there is a way by which all children may become kings, and wear crowns. What kind of crowns? Are they made of gold and jewels? No; but of something that is more precious than gold, and more beautiful than gems and diamonds. And are they just the size for little heads, and may any one wear them that pleases? Yes, they are of all sizes — even for the smallest; and here let me whisper a secret in your ear—*the smallest crowns are always the best.* That is, the sooner you win and wear one, the brighter it is sure to be.

2

I. One of these crowns is *Self-Government.* Oh, how bright and beautiful it is
upon the head of a child, or youth! It needs
no gaudy glitter of jewelry, for it has the
" ornament of a meek and quiet spirit, which
in the sight of God, is *of great price.*" It
is nobler to wear this than to be king.over
many cities and empires; for the wisest
king who ever lived has said, " He that is
slow to anger is better than the mighty;
and he that ruleth his spirit than he that
taketh a city."

I will show you this crown by telling you
a little story of a king who began to reign
when he was ten years old. He became a
Christian, and had a new heart, and loved
the Saviour. But his younger brother, who
was only eight years old, did not believe
that his heart had been changed; and how
do you think he tried to find out whether
his brother was a Christian? Why, he
remembered that whenever he used to tread

on his brother's toes, or plague him in any
way, he would at once become very angry.
and begin to fight him. So, every time he
could get a chance, he would slyly kick him,
or strike him, or pinch his arms, and then
watch to see his face turn red, and his eyes
flash with anger. But with all that he could
do, he could not make him mad. Why was
this? Because he had learned to *rule his
spirit*, and to be king over his angry passions, which before that had been king over
him. No doubt there was many a little
struggle in his breast, but it was the struggle for his crown, and every new triumph
over his temper put a new gem into that
crown, and made it shine brighter and
brighter. And this was the way that he
began to reign when he was ten years old.

Now, when his little brother saw that he
did not get angry any more, it was like seeing the glory of the new crown upon his
heart; 'and then he began to seek after it,

too, and to seek after God until he found
Him—and then there were *two* little kings
in that family.

This, then, is what is meant by ruling the
spirit. It is to govern that busy crowd of
thoughts, feelings, passions, wishes, which,
like a great multitude of people, or like the
different parts of a kingdom, dwell together
in the empire of your heart. That heart,
until it is changed, is full of all sorts of
rebels, such as anger, fretfulness, pride,
malice, and envy. Every one of these tries
hard to become your master. See that boy
who has lost his temper, and who is fretful
and peevish at every thing around him. He
is like a king who has thrown away his
crown, and all the wicked passions in his
breast are fighting together to see which
one shall have it, and rule over him. But is
it not much better that he should be their
master than that they should be his?

" Bertie, dear Bertie, will you not say

good night to me ?" pleaded the sweet voice of his sister Minnie, as she wound her arms lovingly around his neck.

" No," he replied angrily, pushing her away from him.

" Come, now, Bertie, do forgive me, and let us kiss and be friends; will you not, Bertie, dear ?"

He did not answer, but only looked sulkily out of the window. Minnie's blue eyes filled with tears. " You know I did not spoil your kite on purpose, dear brother," she said ; " but it is my bed-time, and if you will not forgive me, I must pray to God ;" and the child left the room. Five minutes after, she was kneeling in her little chamber praying. "Dear, kind Saviour," she said, " do, please, make dear Bertie forgive me. I am so sorry I made him angry, but I did not mean to do so. Pour into his heart Thy Holy Spirit, and let him love me again ; and may he grow up a great and good man, and
2*

be a comfort to dear mamma. Dear Jesus, please hear me, though I am a wicked, sinful child, and make us live very happily together on earth ; and when Thou seest fit, grant that we may meet at Thy great white throne, where all is peace and love, and join dear papa in singing Glory, Glory, Glory." After this prayer, she fell into a sweet sleep.

But Bertie did not sleep well that night, for his conscience troubled him. Early in the morning he went to ask his sister's pardon. Alas! *Minnie was dead.* " Oh, mamma, mamma," cried Bertie, " will she *never* speak to me again ? Shall I *never, never* see her more ?"

" I trust so, my boy ; dear Minnie is only gone before ; will you not try to walk in her footsteps ?"

" Oh, I can never go to her, mamma ; I am a naughty, wicked, selfish boy, and she was so good and gentle. Mamma, I would not say good night to her last evening ;"

and he hid his face on his mother's shoulder, and cried as if his heart would break. Then mother and child knelt down together by the cold form of little Minnie, and prayed, oh, how earnestly! that God would help Bertie to govern his temper. And soon Bertie found this crown, and he grew up to be a good and great man. But never could he think of his last words to his little sister without reproaching himself bitterly.

Now, remember, dear children, whenever you are tempted to be angry, that you may say or do that which you will mourn over as long as you live. Remember that to lose your temper is to throw away your crown ; but that to be mild, and loving, and forgiving, as Jesus was, is to be a true king or queen.

II. Another crown is *Wisdom*. What does King Solomon say about wisdom ? "She shall give to thine head an ornament of grace : a *crown of glory* shall she deliver unto thee."

" A crown of glory !" What little head would not love to wear it ? But this is a crown that is worn *inside* the head—not on the outside ; and its bright jewels are knowledge, prudence, and humility. See that poor boy who works hard all day at making shoes. In front of him is fastened a book, and while his fingers toil so swiftly for his daily bread, his mind toils in patient study ; and all the time the things which he learns are weaving themselves together into a bright crown of wisdom, that shines in everything that he says and does. The people see it and admire it, and ask him to govern their affairs, and the little studious shoemaker becomes the great *Roger Sherman*, of whom many of you have heard or read. Only think of it, dear children ; when you feel like staying from school, or neglecting your lesson, you are throwing away the precious crown of wisdom, without which you never can become truly great or honored in this world.

But is this the whole of the crown that I am now speaking of? No; it has a still brighter jewel, for Solomon says again, " *The fear of the Lord* is the beginning of wisdom." It is a great thing to have the mind filled with all other kinds of knowledge; but the best crown of all is to know, and love, and serve God. For this reason, no other book can make you so wise as *the Bible* can make you. Read it every morning and night, study it, pray over it, saying, " O Lord, open thou mine eyes, that I may behold wondrous things out of Thy law !" If you do this, you shall behold things wonderful indeed— crowns, thrones, diadems—*for you.* And then God will take the pure crown of piety and place it upon your heart, and make you as happy as any king can be. For it is the voice of heavenly wisdom, waiting to crown you, that says, "I love them that love me, and they that seek me early shall find me."

III. Another crown is *obedience to God*. But I hear you say, kings are masters, and not servants. Still, it is a more glorious thing to obey God than it would be to govern all mankind : for at the day of judgment Christ will say to all those who have served Him here, " Well done thou good and faithful servant ; thou hast been faithful over a few things, I will make thee *ruler over many things ;* enter thou into the joy of thy Lord." But before we can reach that joy, we must humbly bow our heads, and let the king put upon them this crown of obedience to Him. I suppose some children think that this is more like a chain or fetter than like the crown of a king : it comes so hard to obey God in all things. But this is only because they have not learned to *love* God ; for to His friends and children

His "yoke is easy," and His "burden is light."

Let us learn a lesson about this from the angels. They obey God always, and do you think that they are unhappy? A Sunday-school teacher, who was talking with his class about that part of the Lord's Prayer which says, "Thy will be done on earth as it is in heaven," said to them, "You have told me, my dear children, what is to be done—the 'will' of God; and where it is to be done—'on earth;' and how it is to be done—'as it is done in heaven.' Now, how do you think that the angels and the happy spirits do the will of God in heaven?"

The first child answered, "They do it directly;" the second, "they do it diligently;" the third, "they do it always;" the fourth, "they do it with all their heart;" the fifth, "they do it all together." Here there was a little pause, and no other child appeared to have an answer, but after some time a lit-

tle girl, who had been thinking deeply, said,
" Why, sir, they do it *without asking any
questions.*"

And she was right; for this is the true
way to mind what God says, without asking
" why ?" or " when ?" or saying, " I don't
want to do it now." If you would be happy
as an angel, then, just as soon as you know
what God commands you, *do it*, no matter
what may happen.

While I am writing these words, there is
a great general at Washington, who has the
command of all the soldiers in this country.
When he was a boy, his wicked father often
made him work in the harvest field on Sunday. But Henry knew when he did so that he
was disobeying God. At last he could stand
it no longer ; and one Sunday, after he had
been working about an hour, he returned
home and told his father that he could not do
so wicked a thing as to work on Sunday, and
he should not do it any more. His father

became very angry, and drove him from the house ; and the brave boy who had dared to lose his home for the sake of obeying God, went out into the wide world with nothing but his little bundle of clothing. But God takes good care of those who serve Him, and he did not let Henry suffer. He grew up to be a good, and wise, and brave man, and now the people everywhere love to honor him. But none of his honors can shine more brightly than this one of *obedience to God*, which the grace of his heavenly Father put upon him when he was fifteen years old.

Who of you, dear children, will have *this* crown ? It may seem hard to get, but oh, it is well worth the winning.

IV. Another crown, beautiful and bright as if it had come straight down from heaven, is that of LOVE.

It *has* come down from heaven · and oh, how sweetly it shines when God sets it on

3

the forehead of a child. It is not, as you
may suppose, an *invisible* crown, for it seems
to let out its soft light from the heart through
all its little windows. It sparkles in the
eyes; it glistens in the smile; it beams in
the actions, and it makes the homeliest face
radiant as the face of an angel. It lights
up the most dreary home, and makes it beautiful and pleasant; and if this crown were
to be taken away from the hearts that wear
it, this world would be a greal deal darker
than it is.

This crown has *two great jewels*, that are
brighter than the most famous diamonds ever
worn by king or queen. These are *Love to
God* and *Love to one another*.

Nothing can be more precious than *love to
God and Christ*. Does it seem hard to love
God, whom you cannot see? Let me tell
you how you may do this. A little girl was
once talking with her mother about those
kind words of Jesus, " Suffer little children

to come unto me;" and she asked, "Does 'come unto me' mean *dying*, mamma?"

"Don't you love and think a great deal about your papa, when he is away?" asked her mother.

"Yes, mamma; I *feel full of papa* sometimes," answered Jessie, "I love him so dearly."

"It is not necessary to see and be with him to love him."

"No, mamma, for he is in my heart really," said the little girl.

"That is what the Lord Jesus means when He asks you to come to Him. It is not to go where He is, in body, but it is to love Him, have your heart *full* of Him, that makes Him near to you, and you near to Him. And it is *so sweet* to come to Him, for He forgives our sins, and takes away our naughty wilfulness, and helps us correct our faults, and makes us love to do right, and love each other and everybody."

"Then I want to come to Jesus; *I wasn't
quite ready to leave you and papa,*" whispered the child.

Now, this is just what God wants you to
do, to *feel full of* your heavenly Father,
and let him have so much room in your
heart that you will love Him more dearly
than any tongue can tell. If you have this
love you will be king indeed; for God will
love you, and bless you, and give you the
kingdom.

What is the other jewel in this crown of
love? It is shown to us in those words of
John, "Little children, *love one another.*"
Once a dear little girl was asked, "What
makes every body love you so much?" "I
don't know," said she, "unless it is because
I love every body." Was it not a beautiful
and true answer? So, let your hearts be
brimfull of love to every body, and you will
be surprised to find how the glory of this
crown-jewel will shine out upon every one

who comes near to you, and will make them all your friends. Then you will do good to others, and they will do good to you; and this love to God and one another will make a little heaven wherever you go.

V. I must tell you of one more crown: and it is as bright as all the others melted into one can make it—"*the crown of glory that fadeth not away.*"

No earthly eye has seen it: for it is so dazzling that these eyes would be blinded by the sight. No mind of man has dreamed of its wondrous glories: for it is grander and more beautiful than these minds can bear to think of. I could describe to you the crown worn by the queen of England, or by the emperor of France; but no words can tell you the splendor of that crown which many a child is now wearing in heaven. I can only say that it is a crown of *Victory;* for they to whom it is given

3*

have conquered sin and Satan and the
grave. It is a crown of *Life;* for they
who wear it shall never die any more. It
is a crown of *Righteousness;* for it shows
that all guilt has been washed from the
heart by the blood of Jesus. And it is a
crown of *Glory:*—but what do you or I
know about the glory that "*shall be re-
vealed?*" We must wait for the hand of
death to uncover it to us. Yet sometimes
the glory seems to shine just a little across
the dark valley.

A few years ago the large factories in the
city of Lawrence, Massachusetts, fell to the
ground, and a great many poor women and
children were buried under them. Among
these were three little Irish girls, who had
learned some of the sweet hymns which they
had heard at the Sabbath-school, and had
also taught them to their little friends.
They lay under the fallen timbers, unable to
move, when suddenly a fire broke out near

them, and they knew that they would be
burned to death before any help could come.
What did they do? They commenced *singing* with all their might,

" I want to be an angel, and with the angels stand,
A crown upon my forehead, a harp within my hand "

Sweetly their voices rose above the crack-
ling of the flames, as they sung through all
the hymn, and then they were heard again
singing joyfully,

" We're going home to glory,"

until their voices were silenced by death.
No, *not silenced*, for as their spirits went up
in that chariot of fire to heaven, and bowed
before the throne to receive their crowns of
glory, although those on the earth could no
longer hear them, the angels heard them
singing " the song of Moses and the Lamb."

Now, dear children, *who wants a crown?*
I think I hear many little voices answering,
" I," and " I," and " I." Well, are you ready

to begin to *win them?* Josiah began to reign in Jerusalem when he was eight years old; but you, though you may be ever so young, may begin *to-day* to wear the crowns of self-government, of wisdom, of obedience. of love, and may wear at last in the *New* Jerusalem, the crown of life and of glory. But to win these crowns, you must do as Josiah did. " *While he was yet young,* he began to seek after God." Then seek Him now, with all your hearts, for He says " They that seek me *early,* shall find me."

II.

The Shepherd.

"Great Shepherd of the sheep,
  Who all Thy flock doth keep,
    Leading by waters calm,
  Do Thou my footsteps guide
  To follow by Thy side:
    Make me Thy little lamb.

" I fear I may be torn
  By many a sharp set thorn
    As far from Thee I stray;
  My weary feet may bleed,
  For rough are paths which lead
    Out of Thy pleasant way.

" But when the road is long,
  Thy tender arm and strong
    The weary one will bear;
  And Thou wilt wash me clean,
  And lead to pastures green,
    Where all the flowers are fair,—

" Till, from the soil of sin
  Cleansed and made pure within,
    Dear Saviour, whose I am,
  Thou bringest me in love
  To Thy sweet fold above,
    A little snow-white lamb."

(33)

The Shepherd.

"He shall feed His flock like a shepherd: He shall gather the lambs with His arms, and carry them in His bosom."—ISAIAH xl. 11.

I LATELY saw a very beautiful sight: *a flock of sheep fed by their shepherd.* And I did not go to the fields or the hills to see it · it was in God's house; in those very seats where you so often sit. Oh, how delightful it was! They came there tired and hungry, and thirsty, and the shepherd spread for them a glorious feast, and while their mouths fed upon the bread and wine, their faith (which might be called the *soul's mouth*) fed upon the body and blood of Jesus; that is, received Him to their hearts as their own crucified Saviour; and they went away satisfied and refreshed.

And I thank God that there were some dear lambs of the flock there too, and that the great heavenly Shepherd fed them as well as the sheep at His table.

But now it is the *lambs' turn;* and I hope that while I talk with you, the great Shepherd will feed your souls with sweet, precious truths, yes, with angels' food, and take you in His strong arms of love, and press you so close to His great, kind heart, that you will be able to understand what the prophet Isaiah means in this beautiful verse. As you look at it in your Bibles, and try to find out what it means, you will be likely to ask three questions about it:

I. *Who is the Shepherd here spoken of ?*

II. *Who are the lambs?*

III. *What is meant by the Shepherd's gathering the lambs with his arm and carry-ing them in His bosom ?*

I hope you will all listen while I try to answer these three questions.

I. First, then, *Who is the Shepherd?*

A great many years before this verse was written, a boy, whose parents lived in Bethlehem in Judea, was sent by his father to tend his flocks of sheep in the pasture. He soon came to love the sheep, and to love the lambs as they frisked and played about him, and ate the tender grass out of his hand ; and as he grew up to be a young man, he took great care of them, kept them from wandering away or being killed by wild beasts, and loved to find out the greenest pastures, and the purest, stillest waters for them, and was in every way a good, kind shepherd.   But God called him away from his flocks. and made him a king.   Yet David did not forget how he had tended the flocks, and he thought to himself, just as

4

I was to my sheep, so the Lord is to me. And then he wrote and sang that sweet Psalm, "*The Lord is my Shepherd*, I shall not want; He maketh me to lie down in green pastures, He leadeth me beside the still waters."

A long time after this, God looked down and saw that His people were straying away from Him, and He said, "I will both search my sheep and seek them out." . . . "*And I will set up one Shepherd over them, and He shall feed them.*" And then again, God said through the prophet Zechariah, "Awake, O sword against my shepherd, . . . *smite the Shepherd*, and the sheep shall be scattered." What? does David say that *the Lord* is his Shepherd, and then another say that He is to be *smitten, killed?* What does this mean? Now, if you will turn to the book of John, you will find out; for there you will hear *Christ* say, "I am the good Shepherd. . . . The good Shepherd layeth down His life for the sheep." And because Jesus is God, and yet was crucified for man, you will see that David was right, and Zechariah was right too, and that they both pointed, just as Isaiah points in our text, to *the Lord Jesus Christ;* and therefore, that He is the good Shepherd who feeds the flock, and takes such tender care of the little lambs. So your first question is answered.

II. Your second question is, *Who are the lambs?*

Let me answer this by telling you a short story.

There was a little girl whose name was Anna, who was called a good girl, and was very much loved. She tried always to please her parents, and to be kind to those about her, and always remembered her prayers morning and night. But Anna had not yet given her heart to the Saviour,

though her mother often told her of Jesus,
and hoped and prayed that she might early
learn to love Him.   One day she brought
home from the Sabbath-school a book called
"The Lambs of Christ's Flock."   At this
time Anna was seven years old.

As her mother read it to her she seemed
to swallow every word of it, and would
often ask, "Am I a lamb of Christ's flock?"
and as her mother read on, she would ask
again and again, the scalding tears rolling
down her face, "Am I a lamb of Christ's
flock, mother?"   Her mother told her she
hoped that she would become one, but this
did not satisfy her.   "Am I one *now?*" she
asked.

"Anna," said her mother, "your heart is
full of sin; you must give your sinful heart
to God, and ask Him for Christ's sake to
wash it from its sin."

"How shall I give my heart to God?
Do please tell me how to give my heart to

Him, I would give my heart to Him, if I only knew how," said Anna.

"Give it to Jesus, just as it is, dear child ; tell Him it is wicked and full of sin, and ask Him to cleanse it in His own precious blood."

"But I am so wicked," said the child, "I am afraid Jesus will not receive me."

"Christ Jesus came into the world to save sinners, to save you, my child," said her mother, "you must give up *all* to Him."

So several days passed away before little Anna found any peace ; but every day she wept and prayed. She wanted, O so much, to be a lamb of Christ's flock.

One afternoon Anna came to her aunt; the tears were all gone, and her eyes were beaming with joy. "Aunty," she said, "I feel *so happy*." Her aunt asked her what made her feel happy. With reverence she answered, "It is God, aunty. He has given me a new heart, and I can trust Him now." Every

4*

night when she went to rest the tears would fill her eyes, as she said, " O, mother, I am afraid I have done something wrong to-day." She was afraid to sin even in thought, and tried in all things to please Jesus, for she felt that now she was His own dear lamb.

Yes—*the children who love the Saviour* are Christ's lambs. *The Church* is His great flock that He is all the time tending and like every other flock it has its *little ones* who belong to the same Shepherd, and need His tender care.

And they are not only called lambs because they are young and small, but because they are *weak and ignorant*. What can be more helpless than a little lamb when any danger is near, without its shepherd? If a wolf or a bear break into the fold, it cannot resist him or run away from him, but must be devoured. It is the same with you, dear children; you are weak, and there are many dangers all around you, and what can you do without Jesus? Why, the strongest sheep in all the flock can do nothing without Him, and how can the feeble *lambs?*

And suppose the lamb gets *lost*, and strays away among the mountains, can it find the way back *alone?* Oh, no; it is ignorant and foolish, and if the shepherd does not go after it and bring it back, it will be sure to perish. Now, how is it with these *human* lambs? Isaiah says, "All we like sheep have gone astray;" and you know that wherever the sheep go, the lambs are sure to follow. David says that we go astray *as soon as we are born.* By this he means that even young children are wicked and sinful; that they go away from God, away from their Shepherd, away from the pleasant pasture grounds of sweet, heavenly truth, away into paths of sin, and danger, and death, and, like the lamb lost in the mountains, you *cannot find the way back alone.* If the Shepherd Jesus does not seek you out, and take you in His arms, then you will never reach the sweet fields of heaven, where the Saviour leads His flock to living fountains of water. But Christ has come " to seek and to save that which was lost;" and when he hears a child praying earnestly to Him for help, and confessing its wickedness, it is like the lamb bleating for its shepherd, and he takes it up in His arms, and folds it to His bosom, and then that child is *Christ's lamb*, and does not wander any more.

But there is another thing in which good children are like lambs. Did you ever see a lamb *quarrel or fight?* No; how gentle, and kind, and loving they are! If they could speak, I am sure they would not utter an angry word. And this is one reason why Jesus is called the Lamb of God—because He is so meek and forgiving. When

you read the story of His death, does it not
make you think of what the prophet said,
" He is brought as a lamb to the slaughter,
and as a sheep before her shearers is dumb,
so He openeth not His mouth"? Now, as it
was with Him, *God's Lamb*, so it should be
with those children who are *Christ's lambs*.
But I have seen boys and girls who were
more like wolves and tigers; so quarrel-
some and fretful that they make themselves
and all around them miserable.

And how *obedient* the lamb is! how it
follows the good shepherd wherever he
leads it; for it knows his voice. So
Christ's lambs will follow and obey Him,
and they are never so happy as when
they are close by His side or in His
arms.

III. I have answered your second question—Who are the lambs?—and there is
only one question left: *What is meant by*

the Shepherd's gathering them with His arms, and carrying them in His bosom?

1. One thing that it means is, that He will *protect them from all danger.* One day when David was tending his flock in a place near the woods, suddenly there came a great lion, and seized a lamb in his teeth, and ran off with it; and I suppose that in a very few minutes he would have eaten it up. What did David do? He started after the lion and smote him, and caught the lamb out of his mouth. And then the lion, who was very angry, sprang with all his might upon David. But David was strong, and the Lord was with him, and he caught the lion by the mane with one hand, and with the other he killed him with his spear, and then carried the lamb back safe and sound to the pasture. Was not that a brave and noble deed?

Now, suppose that this minute just such a great, fierce lion should come and seize one

of these dear lambs, and carry it off to eat—
how frightened we all should be! But
there is one who is worse than a lion, and
stronger than any of the wild beasts you
have ever seen at the menagerie. You can
not see him, nor hear him roar, but he wants
to seize you, and take you away to his
awful den, and devour you. I mean that
terrible being, who, the Bible says, "goeth
about as a roaring lion, seeking whom he
may devour." It is *Satan*, who wants to
destroy us all, and *will do it* too, if God
don't prevent him. I am sorry to say that
there are some who seem hardly to know
or care whether he has them or not. Just
as a man in Africa, Dr. Livingstone, was
once overtaken by a lion, who threw him
down, and he said that, somehow, while the
lion's great paw was upon him, he lost all
fear, and hardly cared whether he was
eaten alive or not. But presently the lion
was shot by another man, and he was glad

enough to escape. So I sometimes think that when this great destroyer has his paw upon the breast of a man or child, they, somehow or other, though it seems very strange, *do not think of their danger.*

But will Christ let him seize and carry off one of *His lambs?*   Oh, no ; He will do as David did : He will snatch away the dear child, even if it is already in Satan's mouth, and take it up, all weak and trembling as it is, and let it rest upon His bosom, where no beast of prey can ever harm it.   For Christ has fought with Satan and conquered him.   He has done more for you and me than David did for his lamb, for He has laid down His life for us that He might deliver us from all evil.

2. Another thing that Christ does for His lambs is to *feed them.*

Once there was a miser, (a hard-hearted, cruel man, who had a great deal of money, but who had not learned how to enjoy it by

making other people happy,) who was overtaken by a violent storm of snow and wind,
and he stopped at the door of a miserable
little cottage that he owned, for shelter.
But he did not go in, and while he stood
there, he heard two children talking together.

"I am hungry, Nettie," said one of them.

"So am I," said the other; "I've been
looking for some potato parings, and I can't
find any."

"What an awful storm!" said the first
one.

"Yes," said Nettie, "the old tree is blown
down; I think God took care it did n't fall
on the house; if it had, it would have
killed us."

"And if He did that, couldn't He send
us *bread?*"

"I'm sure He could. Let us pray 'Our
Father.' and when we come to that part
about *bread*, stop till we get some."

5

So they began, and the miser, shivering outside, listened. When they said " Give us this day our daily bread," and stopped, expecting, in their childish faith, that the bread would come, a kind feeling stole into his mind, and his heart was touched and softened. He had bought a loaf at the village, and he opened the door very softly and threw it in, and then listened to the childrens' cry of delight.

"It dropped right from heaven; did n't it?" said the younger.

" Yes ;" said Nettie, "I shall love God forever, He is so good! He has given us bread because we asked Him."

" We'll ask Him every day, won't we? why, I never thought God was so good, did you?"

" Yes, I always thought so," was Nettie's answer, " but *I never quite knew it before.*"

The storm passed, and the miser went home a better and happier man ; and when, a few weeks afterwards, he died, he gave the little cottage and garden to the father of these praying children. And the little children ever after felt a sweet and solemn feeling when in their prayers they came to those words, " *Give us this day our daily bread.*"

But Christ's lambs have *souls* to be fed as well as bodies. You remember the story of Peter who denied his Lord, and was afterwards very sorry for it. One day Jesus said to him, "Lovest thou me?" "Yea, Lord," he said, "Thou knowest that I love Thee." Then Jesus said to him, "*Feed my lambs.*" What did He mean by this? Why, that Peter, and all Christ's ministers, and all who love Christ, should feed *the souls* of the dear children—that is, teach them about God and heaven. And how can we feed them? Why, out of the Bible; for the Bible was made for the children as well as for the fathers and mothers. And

this is what your teachers are doing in the
Sabbath-school, and your mothers at home,
and what your pastor is doing when he
preaches to you. Do you know that the
word pastor means "shepherd"? That is,
the minister is a kind of under-shepherd,
feeding and tending the sheep and the
'lambs for Christ.' And so the *church* is
your pasture ground, and the *Sabbath-school*
is your pasture ground, where the **Good**
Shepherd feeds you. But oh, remember
that if the lamb *does not eat* the tender
grass, it will do him no good, but he will
grow lean and poor, and then die. So you
must receive all this sweet truth of the
Bible—(David calls it "sweeter than hon-
ey,") — into your minds and hearts, must
learn it, and often think of it, and never
forget it, or *your souls* will starve and die.

3. Another thing that the Lord Jesus
does with His lambs is *to take them in His
arms to heaven when they die* How beautiful

those words of David are, in the Twenty-
third Psalm, where, after speaking of the
"green pastures," and "still waters," he
says, "Yea, though I walk through *the valley
of the shadow of death*, I will fear no evil, for
Thou art with me, Thy rod, and Thy staff
they comfort me!"

Do you know, dear children, that you
must all pass through that valley? I look
forward, and see you lying upon beds of
sickness, the roses fading out of your cheeks,
and the eyes, that now sparkle so brightly,
growing dull and heavy, and your voices,
that now sing so sweetly, becoming silent.
And then, though the sun may shine, and
the flowers bloom as brightly as ever, you
will not see them, nor see the faces of your
parents, brothers and sisters; but you will
be in the dark valley of death. When this
will be, no one knows except God; but I
know and you know that many little feet
enter the valley. Oh, how sad it would be

5*

for any of these dear children to have to pass through it *alone*, with no Shepherd to uphold and comfort them!

But Jesus does not leave His lambs to go through the valley alone; for while He *leads* the sheep with His rod and staff, He takes the weak little lambs *right up in His arms*, and presses them close up to His great, warm, loving heart, and keeps them there till they are safe out of the dark, in the sweet light of heaven, where "everlasting spring abides, and never withering flowers." And what a happy thing it is not to be afraid to die, but to say to Jesus, "*I will fear no evil, for Thou art with me!*" Now if you will give your hearts to Christ, you will be able to say this.

There was once a class of little girls about four years old, in a Sabbath-school, who learned for their lesson the 23d Psalm, "The Lord is my Shepherd." A little girl, who was much younger than they, and

could not speak plain, heard some of them
repeat it at home, and thought that she must
learn, it too. So they said it over to her
till she knew it all by heart; and she loved
it so much that she could hardly think or
speak of anything else all that day. When
her mamma came home, she repeated it to
her, and said, "Mamma, do you know about
the little lambs when they go through the
valley? it is all dark, and the Shepherd takes
them up in His arms and carries them."
In a little while she gave all her heart to
Jesus, and felt that she was one of His
lambs, and that she loved her Shepherd,
and the Shepherd loved her. One day she
said, "Jesus died for us, and we ought to
love Him, and we do love Him, don't we,
mamma?" And she would often throw her
arms around her mother's neck, and say,
"Now tell me about Jesus!" One day her
mother heard her saying, earnestly, "Go
away! go away!" and asked her whom she

was talking to. " I was telling Satan to go away," said she, "and I told Jesus, my Shepherd, to come to me."

After two short years from the time she had learned the little Psalm, Clara passed through the dark valley. Was she afraid? No; she feared no evil, but with a happy smile kissed her father and mother "good-bye," and her spirit sprang into the arms of Jesus, and nestled lovingly upon His bosom And although many tears fell over that cold little form, her parents knew that her soul was safe through the valley, and that they should meet Clara again upon the other side. Yes,

> " The pearly gates were opened,
>   And glowing seraphs smiled,
>   And with their tuneful harp-strings
>   Welcomed the little child.
>
> " They shouted ' High and Holy !
>   A child has entered in !

And now from all temptation
A soul is sealed from sin.'

" They led her through the golden streets,
On toward the King of kings,
While the glory fell upon her
From the rustling of their wings.

" The Saviour smiled upon her
As none on earth had smiled,
And heaven's great glory shut around
The little earth-born child.

" On earth they missed the little one,
They sighed and wept and sighed,
And wondered if another such
As their's had ever died

" Oh, had they seen through those high gates
The welcome to her given,
They never would have wished their child,
Back from her home in Heaven !"

Dear children, will you not become the
lambs of Christ, that He may protect, and
feed, and comfort you while you live, and

make you happy with Him forever? Oh,
how glad Jesus would be to take you up in
His arms and bless you! Hark! do you
hear that voice? Listen a moment with the
ear of your heart. Is not some one calling
you? Don't you hear Jesus saying, " Suffer
little children to come unto me, and forbid
them not, for of such is the kingdom of
heaven"? "I love them that love me, and
they that seek me early shall find me"? *It
is the Good Shepherd*, asking you to become
His lambs! Why don't you fall right into
His arms and sing, " *The Lord is my Shepherd*"?

In the gospel by Luke, Jesus tells us a
beautiful parable about a man who had a
hundred sheep, and one of them strayed
away and was lost. What did he do?
leave it to die? No; he left all the rest
of the flock, and hastened over the hills,
and through the valleys, until at last he
found it, and put it on his shoulders, and

carried it all the way back. Then he called his neighbors and friends together, and said to them, " Rejoice with me, for I have found my sheep which was lost." Now Jesus explains this parable by saying that in the same way there is "joy in heaven over one sinner that repenteth."

So, when one of these children becomes Christ's lamb, the Lord Jesus says to His holy angels, "Rejoice with me, for I have found my lamb which was lost!" and then they all strike their golden harps, and sing together, oh, how sweetly, over the glad news that a child has given its heart to God.

Oh, that they and we could have such glad news to sing over now! And shall we not?

III.

The Crowned Flock.

" A LITTLE.flock ! So calls he thee,
    Who bought thee with his blood ;
  A little flock,—disowned of men,
    But owned and loved by God.

" But the chief Shepherd comes at length;
    Thy feeble days are o'er ;
  No more a handful in the earth,
    A little flock no more.

" No more a lily among thorns,
    Weary, and faint, and few,
  But countless as the stars of heaven,
    Or as the early dew.

" Unfading palms they bear aloft ;
    Unfaltering songs they sing ;
  Unending festival they keep
    In presence of their King."

The Crowned Flock.

"Fear not, little flock, for it is your Father's good pleasure to give you the Kingdom."—LUKE xii. 32.

IN a great wild desert, which is full of howling beasts, there lives a little flock of sheep and lambs. They often tremble for fear that they will be torn in pieces by the fierce lions and tigers that roar angrily around them, and glare on them from their dens, but they press close up to the Shepherd's side, and are safe from harm. And, strange enough, these sheep and lambs are *all princes;* for their Shepherd is also a King, and He has a crown and a kingdom for every one of them. How wonderful! Who ever heard of such a thing as sheep and lambs wearing *crowns?*

Now, you will understand what I have

said, when I tell you that the great desert
is this world, and the wild beasts are Satan
and wicked men, and the little flock are
those who love Jesus Christ, and their kingdom is heaven.   So that our text means
just this—that although Christ's friends are
very few and small and weak, and there is
a great deal to make them afraid, yet they
must not fear, because their heavenly Father
will be sure to give them the kingdom.

Although these words were spoken by
Jesus to *all* His disciples, whether old or
young, I remember, as I look at them, that
He once took children in His arms and said,
" Of such is the kingdom of heaven ;" and
I know, from that sweet saying, that He
means this message just as much for the
lambs as for the sheep.   And so I think I
now hear His kind voice saying to you who
are his friends, " Fear not, little flock, for it
is your Father's good pleasure to give you
the kingdom."

Those children that love the Saviour are a "*little* flock" of Jesus.   They are not only small and weak and tender, but are also little in *numbers* as well as in size. Although there are a great many children in the world, how few there are who love and obey God!   I wonder how many of the dear children who read these pages can say, *from the heart*, "The Lord is my Shepherd."   Only a very few, I fear, though I wish that you *all* could do so ; for none are so happy as the little flock of Christ.   As I have already shown you, they have many pleasures and comforts here : but the best of all is this—that they are to be crowned with such glory hereafter.

I. As we now listen together to the Shepherd's kind voice, let us look, first of all, at the *precious gift* of the Father which He here tells us of : " It is your Father's good pleasure to give you *the kingdom*."

6*

You see that Christ does not here say, "*a* kingdom," nor tell what kind of a kingdom it is, nor where it is; but says, "*the* kingdom," as if there were only one worth having, and as if His disciples knew all about it already. What, then, can it be, and where is it to be found?

You will not find it on the map of this world. You will see there the kingdoms of Great Britain, and Spain, and Italy, and the empires of France, and Austria, and Russia; but the kingdom of Christ's little flock is greater and more glorious than all those of this world would be if they were put together. For it is *the kingdom of Heaven*, where the Lord Jesus Christ has His splendid throne at the right hand of God the Father, and where all Christ's friends shall live and reign forever. The Bible tells us much about that land of beauty and of glory: how every one who is there is crowned with a golden crown, and plays on a golden harp, and sings the song of Moses and the Lamb ; how they are all clothed in white robes, and carry palms of victory—just as the children in Jerusalem waved the branches of the palm trees when they sang, " Hosanna to the Son of David ;" how the streets are of pure gold, and the walls of precious stones, and the gates of pearl ; how there are no tears there, no pain, no darkness, no sin, no death ; and how the bright, beautiful angels, with their shining wings, and their sweet voices, make every heart glad, and fill the soft air with their music. It is the " Father's House," where there are " many mansions," and where Jesus has gone to " prepare a place " for all who love Him, and where he is leading, step by step, all His " little flock." Oh,

> " Beautiful Zion, built above !
> Beautiful city that I love !
> Beautiful gates of pearly white !
> Beautiful temple—God its light !"
> " There shall my eyes the Saviour see—
> *Haste to this heavenly home with me !"*

Do you remember when, within a few years, the Prince of Wales came across the ocean to visit this country? A great many people rushed to see him, and the newspapers were full of what he said and did, and it seemed as if men could think and talk of nothing else. And why was all this? Because he is the son of a Queen, and, if he lives, will some day have *a kingdom.* But the people need not have gone so far to see a prince. If they had looked at the little flock in the Sabbath-school, or church, they could have seen the *princes of Heaven*, the children of the greatest of all kings, whose heads shall wear brighter crowns, and who shall sit on more glorious thrones than were ever dreamed of in this world. But they are only a "*little* flock," and the world does not see what the angels see, that their heavenly Father is holding out a rich crown over their heads. The world does not crowd to look at you, and feast you, and get up grand processions to honor you, oh child of the kingdom! but never mind—Christ says, " Ye are not of the world, even as I am not of the world," and, " Fear not, little flock, for it is your Father's good pleasure to give you the kingdom." And so, although a child may be ever so poor, and ragged, and despised, and his heart ready to break in this cold, hard world, if he only is one of the " flock," his feet shall yet enter the pearly gates and tread the golden streets on high, and his heart be filled with all the rich joys of heaven.

" Well, I don't know as I was made for anything," said a poor little girl one day, when she thought she was alone by the roadside. She had a miserable, drunken mother, and her brother, who should have been kind to her, was very ugly and cruel. And the tears trickled down, like an April shower, under her little sun-bonnet that she tried to pull over her face to hide them. The

birds were singing about her, and the sun
shining, and the little brook running over
the stones, and the flowers giving their
sweet perfume—all seemed made for something, excepting her, she thought. And she
went on sobbing to herself, "Mother says
I'm always in the way, and always good for
nothing, and Will scolds me all day ; maybe
I was not made for anything. I don't see
what I was put in the world for, then. I
wish I never had been." And she sat down
on a mossy bank by the side of the road,
and cried as if her heart would break, as
she said, " The birds and everything are
made for something ; why wasn't I ? No, I
was not made for anything."

" Yes, little one," said a voice above her,
"you were made for something. *You were
made to be an angel in Heaven.*"

What voice was that ? Was it an angel
sent down from God to comfort the poor
girl ? No ; it was a kind lady ; yet one

whom God had sent to cheer His weeping
lamb. The little girl turned her sad face
toward her and said, "Mother says I was
not made for anything." "But you are,"
said the lady; "you are made to be a
little angel in heaven." "But where is
heaven?" she asked. "Can I go there
now."

And then the lady told her all about that
happy place; and how the blessed Jesus
had left His throne of glory, and came down
upon earth, and took little children in his
arms and blessed them; and how he died a
cruel death, that they might become little
angels in heaven.

Then the little girl dried her tears and
smiled, as she asked, "And can I be a little
angel, too? Oh, how I should love to be
one, and to see Jesus!" The lady told her
she could, if she would love Jesus; and she
gave her a Bible that told her all about
heaven, and how she could get there; and

when, after that, her cruel mother called her
" a good-for-nothing thing," and said she
was ' not made for anything," she would
say softly to herself, " Yes, I was made to
be a little angel in heaven ," and when,
sometimes, she went to bed cold and hungry,
she would look up to the stars ; she thought
they were bright, just like heaven, and that
perhaps the angels were looking down upon
her, and would some day come and take
her away, to be an angel, too, in heaven.

And so you, dear little flock of Jesus,
were " made for something "—made to be
angels, made to wear crowns of glory ; and
if you love the Lord Jesus, and pray to
Him, you may always look up beyond the
stars, and no matter what may trouble you,
may hear the Saviour's voice saying to you,
'' Fear not, little flock, for it is your Father's
good pleasure to give you the kingdom."

II. But I think I hear one of you saying,

How shall I get there? It is such a great, and glorious, and holy kingdom, and I am so poor, and weak, and sinful! Well, let me now show you, in the second place, how, if you love Christ, heaven becomes *your kingdom*. What says our text? " It is your Father's *good pleasure to give you* the king-dom."

To *"give"* it? Why, then we have not got to *buy* it, or to earn it in any way. If your father makes you a present, although it may have cost him ever so many dollars, all you have to do is to reach out your hand and take it. So heaven is a Father's gift, and Jesus Christ is a gift, for " God so loved the world as to *give* His only begotten Son, that whosoever believeth on Him might not perish, but have everlasting life "—that is, might have the kingdom of heaven. All the riches in the world are not enough to buy one of those crowns or harps ; all your good actions could not buy it ; nor all your

7

tears, although you should mourn over your sins forever. But the blood of Christ, which is more precious than all worlds, has bought Heaven for our souls. The good Shepherd has laid down His life for the little flock, and *for the Shepherd's sake* it is the Father's good pleasure to give to that flock " the kingdom." All, then, that you have to do is to come, with sorrow for sin, and with faith in the Lord Jesus, and *take* the glorious gift. If you wait to *earn it*, you must wait for-ever.

Once there was an Indian and a white man, who both began to seek after Heaven at about the same time. The Indian very soon had a good hope of the kingdom, but the white man was a long time without any hope at all. One day they met, and he said to his Indian friend, " How was it that you found comfort so much sooner than I did ?" " Oh, brother," said the Indian, " me tell you. There come along a rich king. He

say He give you new coat. You look at
your coat and say, 'I don't know ; my coat
pretty good. I think it will do a little
longer.' He then offer me new coat. I
look on my old blanket. I say, 'This good
for nothing.' I fling it right away, and take
the beautiful garment. Just so, brother,
you think you pretty well off ; you want to
buy Heaven with your goodness ; but I,
poor Indian, have nothing, and so I glad to
take it all as a gift."

Yes ; we must all come like that poor
Indian, having nothing—must come just as
we are, not waiting to become any better,
and let God *give us* the kingdom.

For, you see by my text that He does not
give it because we are good and holy, but
because of His "*good pleasure ,*" because
He thinks best to give it. And is it not a
delightful thought that it is *a pleasure to
God* to give away the crowns, and robes, and
harps of heaven to His poor little flock, and

that He is just as happy in giving them as
we can be in receiving them?

III. And ought not this thought, (thirdly,)
to *take away all our fears?* O, how com-
forting are these two words of the Shepherd
to His little flock, the children of the kingdom, " *Fear not.*"

There are many things in this world that
are apt to make the lambs of Jesus tremble.
There are sorrows and trials that almost
break the heart; and Satan, like a roaring
lion, tries to devour us before we reach the
kingdom ; and the river of death looks dark
and frightful, and we sometimes almost fear
*t*hat we can never get to that " shining
shore." All this shows how true Paul's
words were when he said that " we must
through much tribulation enter into the kingdom of God." But do we need to be afraid?
No ; for we have an Almighty Father, and
it is His good pleasure to give us the king-

dom, and nothing can prevent Him from doing His pleasure.

Then fear not. The flock may be ever so "little," but God is very great; and heaven may seem a great way off, but your Shepherd is very near. And the way may seem hard and thorny, but Christ will give you strength to travel it. And when death comes, you may look up to the Shepherd, as David did, and say, "I will fear no evil, for Thou art with me."

A little girl whose name was Lillie, stood looking up to the sky when the sun was setting. The clouds were all gold and crimson, such as you have sometimes seen, and she said to her mother, "How beautiful! oh, how I should like to be away up there with the angels!" The mother looked up and answered, "Yes, darling, the clouds are very beautiful to-night." "But, mamma," said Lillie, "do you know what makes them beautiful? I do; it is because the angels

7*

are in them, and I was just thinking that when I died, maybe I would look right down here, mamma, sometime, upon you. Say don't you think I will?"

And then she said, " Mamma, I want to be an angel ; but I don't want to die, as little Bessie died, and be put into the cold ground. You won't let me die, and be buried up, will you, mamma ?"

And the mother wept as she answered, " When the Saviour calls my little lamb, I shall have to give her up. You would be willing to go to Jesus, and never be sick any more, wouldn't you, darling ?"

" Yes, mamma, if He would take me right up to the beautiful sky ; but oh, mamma, I don't want to be put into the ground !"

The mother kissed her trembling child, and said, " Don't you remember the little dark root which you saw me plant right here in the spring ?"

" Yes, mamma, I do ; it came up with

two lovely green leaves, and it grew up into this tall shrub, which has so many beautiful flowers upon it."

"So," said the mother, "we must die and be buried up in the cold ground, that our spirits may rise up as the flowers do above the earth, in beauty and purity to heaven. If we do not die, my child, we can never go to heaven to live with Christ and the angels."

The child looked for an instant upon the flowers, and then exclaimed, with a bright smile, "Oh, mamma, I do not feel afraid now to die and be buried up in the ground, because I shall rise up far more beautiful than I am now, to live away up in the blue sky with Christ and the angels." And when at last her blue eyes closed in death, she whispered, "Mamma, I am not afraid to be put into the ground, for I am going to be an angel."

"Ah, it was the Shepherd's kind voice that spoke to little Lillie, and said to her secret soul, "Fear not, for it is your Father's good pleasure to give you the kingdom."

I will close with the story of another of Christ's flock who was not afraid to die. He was a poor little boy who had to work in the coal mines for a living. One day the gas in the mines took fire, and blew up everything around it, and the workmen were buried under the great stones that it threw upon them. The people at the top went straight to work to find their dead bodies, and among them they found this little boy. There was a painted tin box by his side, and a rusty nail, and on the box were these words which he had scratched there with the nail in the dark, when he felt himself dying: "Fret not, dear mother, for we were singing while we had time, and praising God. Mother, follow God more than ever I did." On the other side of the box he wrote, "Johnny, farewell! Be a good boy to God and thy mother."

When his mother read those words, she knew that her dear boy had not been afraid to die.

Oh, dear children, Christ can take away this and every other fear from every one of you, if you will only become the lambs of His little flock! Will you not do so, that we may go on together to the kingdom, so that when, at last, "the dead, small and great, shall stand before God," we may all, parents and children, teachers and scholars, pastor and people, hear that voice, " Come, ye children of my Father, inherit the kingdom prepared for you from the foundation of the world!"

IV.

The Strong Guide.

" TAKE thy staff, O pilgrim,
    Haste thee on thy way ;
Let the morrow find thee
    Farther than to-day.

"If thou seek the city
    Of the Golden Street,
Pause not on thy pathway,
    Rest not, weary feet.

" In the heavenly journey
    Press with zeal along :
Resting will but weary,
    Running make thee strong.'

The Strong Guide.

"Wilt thou not from this time cry unto me, My Father, Thou art the Guide of my youth?"—JEREMIAH iii. 4.

ONCE there was a little boy, only five years old, who had disobeyed his mother. After he had gone to bed at night, she went softly to his room to talk with him about it, but she found that he had been thinking of his wicked heart, and felt very sorry for what he had done. For, as soon as he saw her coming, he said, "Mother, I wish I was in heaven." "Why so, my dear boy?" asked his mother. "Because," said he, "then I should *know* that I should go to heaven, and now I don't know."

And has not this thought sometimes crossed your minds—what a sweet, happy

8

thing it would be *to know* that when the short journey of life is over, and this body dies, my spirit will rest forever in God's beautiful home?

Now a voice comes to you from that home in the skies, and your kind, loving heavenly Father asks you in my text, to let Him lead you to the happy land. You see He asks you a very solenm question; and it is one that He expects you each one to answer: "Wilt thou not from this time cry unto me, 'My Father, Thou art the guide of my youth?'"

I. That I may help you to answer this question, let me now show you, in the first place, *how much you all need a guide.*

When men are tavelling in the far East, over the burning sands of the desert, (where there are no railroads or stage coaches such as we have,) they go in *caravans*—that is, a great many of them together. Sometimes there will be hundreds of persons, and

thousands of camels, that stretch out in a
long line as far as the eye can see. But
whether there are many or few, they are
always sure to have one man going before
them whom they call the *hybee*, or guide.
If any company of travellers should think
of going over the desert without him, they
would be as foolish as if we were to try to
travel in the railroad cars without a con-
ducter or engineer; and they would be
almost sure to get lost by the way. This
guide must be one who knows all about the
country through which they are to pass.
He must be able to tell when the dreadful
simoom, or hot wind is rising, so that they
may be able to prepare for it. He must
know where the sands are most firm, and
where they are shifting, so that the men
and beasts may not sink in them. He must
know all about the wells and springs by the
way, where they may drink, and not die of
thirst; and where the little oases, that is,

the grassy resting-spots, are found. And he
must be a man who knows the tribes of
Arabs, and can keep them from robbing the
caravan. Every one follows and obeys this
guide, until he has led them safe to the journey's end.

Now, I see before me *a little caravan;*
a company of travellers. And where are
you going? *To eternity.* Some of these
little feet have only begun the journey,
others have been longer on the way. Now
and then one has dropped down by your
side, and you have seen them no more;
they have reached the journey's end before
you. But just as fast as the minutes fly,
you are all going on—on to another world.

And, like the travellers over the desert,
do you not need *a guide?* Oh, yes, for
there are many dangers before you. There
are many wrong paths that do not lead to
heaven, but lead far away from it; paths
pleasant to look upon, but oh, their end is

misery and death. See that boy who is breaking the holy Sabbath. or who is learning to lie, or steal, or swear. He has got into the wrong path, because he has *no guide.* See that girl who disobeys her parents, or who forgets to read her Bible, or pray to God. She is in the wrong path: she needs *a guide.* See that man who is now in jail for murdering another man; do you think his hand could have done such a wicked thing, if, when he was young, he had put it into the hand of the heavenly Father, and said, "Thou art the Guide of my youth"? And you are so weak, and Satan is so strong, and he is trying so hard to lead your steps away from God and heaven, and to trip you up, now by one sin, and now by another—oh, those little feet *cannot go alone* through this wicked world to heaven. When you try to look up and sing of that "happy land," do you not have to say that it is "*far, far away*"? it seems

8*

so distant, and sin and Satan are so near;
it seems so hard to reach, and the wrong
way seems so easy!

Yes, my little pilgrims, you need, and
we all need, a strong, and loving, and
wise *Guide:* one stronger than any man,
and who loves us so well that He will
take us by the hand, and never let us
go away from Him; one who knows where
the springs of living water are; one who
can lift you over the bad places, and lead
your tired feet to pleasant resting-spots,
and who can guide you to the heavenly
home, and not let you get lost by the
way.

But is there anywhere such a guide as
this for little pilgrims? Yes; and see, He
offers Himself to you in our text, and asks
you to make Him *your* Guide.

II. I have shown you how much you all
need Him, and now the second thing I wish

to say is, that *your heavenly Father is just the Guide that you want.*

Suppose you were in a strange place, a great way off from your home, and some one you had never seen or heard of before should offer to take you to your father's house. You would say, " Can I trust him ? How do I know but that he will deceive me and take me where I shall never see my father's face again ?" But if *your father* himself should come, then you would feel safe ; and although the way might seem new, and it might be so dark that you could not see where you were going, you would only keep holding his hand the more tightly, knowing that he would be sure to lead you home.

It is the same with God. He is your Father in Heaven, and He comes down to your heart and says, " My poor, dear child, you are lost. You are a great way off from your Father's house. But I love you still, and I want you to come to my happy home.

Give me that wicked heart, and I will make it good, and fit it to live with angels. Only do as I tell you to do, follow where I lead, and *trust me all the time*, and I will bring you safe home again.

Can you not trust Him? Who knows so much about Heaven as God who has always lived there? Whose eye can so watch over you, and see every danger in your way, and see everything that Satan does to harm you? What arm is so strong to help you in your weakness? and what heart is so kind and pitying as that of the Father in Heaven?

Once there was a strong ship sailing over the ocean, when a terrible storm came on. The winds blew, and the great waves dashed hard against the vessel, and the tall masts cracked, and the passengers were very much frightened, for they thought that they were all going down to the bottom of the sea. But one brave boy was there, and the rest all wondered why his cheek did not turn pale as the others', nor any tears come into his bright eye. They asked him if he was not afraid of the dreadful storm; "No;" said he "for *my father's at the helm.*" His father was guiding the ship, and he trusted in that father's skill, and felt that he knew how to guide it right, so as to bring them all safe to the shore. '

Now this life is like a great sea, and we are all sailing over it—

"Out on the ocean all boundless we ride,"

but oh, are we all " *homeward bound?*" I hope that some of us are ; but that " shining shore " of heaven is hard to reach, and none can get there who try to guide the ship themselves. But if you can say, " *My Father's at the helm,*" then, like the boy I have told you of, you need fear nothing ; for He can guide you through the waves ; and though now you say,

  " Wildly the storm sweeps us on as it roars;
    Look! yonder lie the bright heavenly shores!"

And soon you shall sing,

    " Into the harbor of heaven now we glide,
        We're home at last;
    Softly we drift o'er its bright silver tide,
        We're home at last!

    Glory to God! all our dangers are o'er,
    We stand secure on the glorified shore!
    Glory to God! we will shout evermore—
      We're home at last!"

Oh, blessed home for wearied souls! Oh, kind and loving Father who guides us to it! Wilt thou not from this time cry unto Him, " *My Father, Thou art the Guide of my Youth!*"

Thus a dear little boy in the city of Boston had learned to say to God. He was very sick, and one night he saw something so very beautiful, so like heaven, that when he told it to his parents they thought that God must have given him a little sight of

that happy world before he reached it. He
was very much delighted with what he saw,
but while he was looking at it with his
mind, there seemed to rise up some great
mountains between him and heaven, hiding
it from his sight. This was very sad, but in
a moment his face brightened up again, and
he said, "*A strong man will carry me over
the mountains!*" Ah, he knew that his
Guide was with him, and that he was strong
enough to take his spirit right up over the
mountain of death to the happy home beyond. Then he asked his father and mother
to *go up with him*, and threw his arms
about a young friend's neck, and tried to
lift her, as if he would pull her up with him
from this world to heaven. But it was not
yet time for her to go, although she followed him in a few days; and he went up
alone—no, not alone, for *his Guide* was with
him, and the dear child was soon in the
bosom of its heavenly Father.

And there are many other children and youth who have said to God, "Thou art my Guide," and their Father is leading them, a happy flock, "in ways of pleasantness and paths of peace." They cry, "Our Father which art in heaven;" and He says, "Ye shall be My sons and daughters, saith the Lord Almighty." They cry, "Keep us from temptation, and deliver us from evil," and He sends His angels to encamp around them, and sends His Holy Spirit to keep them from sinning. And a great many of these children of God are growing up to be holy men and women, and they make one large, happy family, and God is all the time bringing them home. Soon our turn will come. Oh, let us be ready, and let us feel every day that God is guiding our feet to Himself. Let us look up and sing,

> " I'm a pilgrim and I'm a stranger,
>   I can tarry, I can tarry but a night.

There's the city to which I journey;
  My Redeemer, my Redeemer is its light.
There is no sorrow nor any sighing,
Nor any tears there, nor any dying."

III. But it is time that I tell you, in the third place, *How the Father guides His Children through this world to heaven.*

Do you say, God is a great way off. I cannot see His face, or hear His voice, or feel his strong hand in mine—how, then, can He be my Guide?

It is true that you cannot see Him with these eyes, nor hear Him with these ears, but is not God all the time speaking to the ear of your heart? Do you not sometimes, when you feel like doing wrong, hear a little voice in your soul that says, "Don't you do it—it's wicked!" That is one of God's voices. We call it *conscience.* A man without a conscience would be like a ship without a rudder, that goes just as the winds and waves carry it, and that is sure to

9

be dashed to pieces. Oh, never disobey that voice within you, for it is one of the ways by which God tries to guide you to heaven.

But we want another and a stronger voice than this, and we have got it. How is God speaking to you in my text? Why, out of *the Bible*. This is as much God's word to you and me as if we could see Him here in all His glory, or stood before His throne' and heard it from his lips. And when you read in your Bibles, " Remember now thy Creator, in the days of thy youth ;" " They that seek me early shall find me," and those words of Jesus, " Suffer little children to come unto me "—then God is showing you the way to heaven. Oh, *love* your Bibles ! read and study them every day ! Try to be *full* of the Bible, and it will be to you just as it was to David, when he said, " Thy word is a lamp to my feet and a light to my path." That is, if your way seems ever so dark, the Bible will make it light again, and keep your feet from stumbling.

I wish you could love your Bibles as two little boys did, who lived in London. Their father and mother both died, and they had no longer any home. So they put their clothes in two little bundles, and started off to walk to Liverpool, a great many miles away, where they had an uncle living. After they had walked all day, they came to a lodging-house, and asked the keeper if they might sleep there, for they had no money to pay him with. But the smallest of the two boys had a Bible in his pocket, and the keeper said to him, "You have no money, and no meat. Will you sell me this Bible? I will give you five shillings for it." The tears rolled down the poor boy's cheeks, and he said, "No; I'll starve first." "Why," said the man, "do you love this Bible so much? What has it done for you?" And then the boy said, "When I

was about seven years old, I became a Sunday scholar in London. I soon learned to
read my Bible. It showed me that I was a
sinner, and a great one, too. It also pointed
me to my Saviour, and I thank God that I
have found mercy at the hands of Christ."
Then the man, to try him still farther, offered
him *six* shillings for the Bible. "No," said
he, "it has been my support all the way
from London. Hungry and tired, I have
often sat down by the way-side to read my
Bible, and have found refreshment from it."
"Well," said the man, "but what will you
do when you get to Liverpool, if your uncle
should refuse to take you in?" His answer
was a noble one: "My Bible tells me that
'when my father and my mother forsake
me, then the Lord will take me up.'" Of
course, the keeper o the house gave the
poor boys their lodging, and the next
morning they set out early on their journey.

Now, just as this young traveller sat down by the roadside, and found such comfort in the Bible, when he was weary, so you, " pilgrims and strangers," may find sweet comfort in it all along your way to the celestial city. Whenever you read its pages, your heavenly Father will talk with you, and show you just the path in which He wants you to go. If you will only love and obey your Guide-book, it will be sure to keep you in the way of life.

IV. But there are three very important words in my text that we must not forget— "from this time." " Wilt thou not *from this time* cry unto Me, ' My Father, Thou art the Guide of my youth ?' "

What does this mean ? Why, that you must not wait till to-morrow, or next week, or next year, to make God your Guide ; but that *now*, just when God speaks to you in

9*

His word, is the time to give your heart up to Him, and say, *Thou art my Guide!*

And why should you not do this? Can you give any good reason why you should let Satan keep you back from Him any longer? I know you cannot. But I know, and you know, that there are the best of reasons why you should come to Him to-day. Oh, there are very many men and women who would tell you that their most bitter sorrow is, that they did not give themselves to God when they were as young as you are. They feel as the poet felt, when he wrote that prayer,

" Restore my youth to me ! O God, restore
   My morn of life ! Oh, Father, *be my Guide,*
   And let me choose my path once more !"

But they cannot choose it again, for we have only one life here. But *you* can to-day choose your path, and choose your Guide. To-morrow may be too late.

God is waiting for your answer. What do you say? Oh, "wilt thou not from this time"—yes, *from this moment*, cry unto Him, "My Father, *Thou art the Guide of my Youth?*"

V.

The Brave Conquerors.

" This life is a battle with Satan and sin,
And we are the soldiers, the victory to win,
   And Christ is the Captain of our little band;
Whatever opposes, for Him we will stand

" To God, for our armour, we'll fail not to go,
He'll clothe us with truth and with righteousness too,
   The "gospel of peace" shall our footsteps attend,
The good "shield of faith" from all harm shall defend.

" Though little temptations (the worst ones of all)
Will often beset us, to make us to fall,
   We'll "stand up for Jesus," and, when life is o'er,
For us He'll be standing on Jordan's bright shore."

The Brave Conquerors.

"And he commanded the most mighty men that were in his army to bind Shadrach, Meshech and Abednego, and to cast them into the burning fiery furnace."—DANIEL iii. 20.

SUPPOSE that some great, wicked heathen king should come with his soldiers to our pleasant homes, and burn our houses, and carry us away to his own country—taking these dear children away from their parents, and the parents away from their children, so that we should never see each others faces any more—how very sad we all should feel!

Now if you read the first chapter of this book of Daniel, you will find a very interesting story of four little boys, who, when they were children, were carried far away from Jerusalem, their home, to the great city of Babylon, by the king Nebuchadnezzar.

And what did he do with them? I suppose a great many of the poor Jews were made servants and slaves, and were very unhappy. They sat down by the rivers of Babylon, and hung their harps upon the willow trees that grew along the banks, and wept when they remembered Zion. They could not sing as they used to do at home, for "How," they asked, "shall we sing the Lord's song in a strange land?"

But this was just what *God had told them* would happen if they did not obey him. And do you not think they felt sorry enough for their sins, when they found themselves carried away into that strange, wicked country?

But what became of the *four little boys?* I hear you ask. Well, God took good care of them, for they had learned to love

God; and, as they were very beautiful and bright, they were taken right to the king's house; and the king gave them wise teachers, and told them to study hard for three years, and then come to him, and he would find out by that time what they were good for.

The three years soon passed away, and then came their *examination-day;* and when they stood before the king, and answered the hard questions that were put to them, he found them, the Bible says, " ten times better than all the magicians and astrologers," that is, all the wise and learned men " that were in his realm." And how did these boys come to know so much? Ah! they were *praying* children, and " *God* gave them knowledge and skill in all learning and wisdom." They *studied* hard, and they *prayed* hard; and I am sure that any boy or girl who tries to learn, and all the time asks God for help, will grow up to be a wise man or woman.

Now, one of these four boys was *Daniel*, the one who was afterwards thrown into the lion's den because he prayed to God, and came out without being hurt; and the other three are the ones spoken of in my text, who were thrown into a fiery furnace. And this is the way it happened:

The king Nebuchadnezzar was what we call *a heathen* — that is, one who worships idols that are made by the hands of men, instead of worshipping the true God—and so were all his people. Well, the king had a great graven image made, all covered over with gold, and it was ninety feet high, so that it could be seen a great way off; and then he had a band of music standing near it, and told all the people that when they heard the band playing they must fall down on the ground and worship it; and that if any of them did not do this, they should be cast into a burning fiery furnace. The people did not know any better, (poor souls, they had never heard about the true God,) and so, when the music sounded, they fell flat on the ground and worshipped the golden image. But did these three boys, (who had now grown up to be young men,) bow down before it? No; they had not forgotten the second commandment which their mothers had taught them when they were little children, and although they knew the king would be angry, and have them thrown into the furnace of fire, they stood right up upon their feet; for they feared God more than man. And as soon as the king heard of it, he called them before him and asked why they had not worshipped the image. But they were not afraid, because they knew that they were doing right; and they answered him, " Our God whom we serve is able to deliver us from the burning fiery furnace, and He

will deliver us out of thine hand, O king."
Was not that a noble answer? But the
king became very angry, and told his servants to heat the furnace seven times hotter
than it was before, and to throw these men
right into it. Oh, how awfully wicked
and cruel men can become who do not
love and serve God! Babylon was like
"the dark places of the earth" that David
speaks of, which he says are "full of the
habitations of *cruelty.*" And oh! there
are a great many such places in the world
now; and I am glad that you are every
Sabbath bringing your pennies to send
them the Bible and the missionary that
they may be made better, and taught to
throw away their images and worship the
true God. *Give* all you can, *pray* all you
can; for there are a great many people
bowing down to-day before idols that their
hands have made, and calling them their
gods!

Did you ever look into the furnace
where they melt the hard iron, and see
the hot flames blazing so furiously, and
the iron poured out like red hot water?
I do not think you would like to go very
near to such a fire as that. And if any one
were to be thrown right into it, how awful
it would be! Only think of it — to be
burned to death! Why, if you happen to
burn your finger you think it is pretty hard
to bear; but it was not the hands or
fingers, but the whole bodies of these young
men that were cast into the furnace! and
the fire was so hot that the men who threw
them in were burned to death for coming
so near to it.

But what became of these three who
were thrown in? I will tell you. The
king came as near as he dared to, and
looked into the furnace, and saw a wonderful sight. There they were walking through
the fire, the flames blazing fiercely all around

them, but neither their clothes nor their hair was even singed by it; and most wonderful of all, though only three were cast in, now there were *four*—and the fourth was *an angel of God*. And then the king told them to come out from the fire; and he worshipped the God who had saved them, and told the people that if any of them should say anything against the God of the Jews, they should be killed; and he made these three young men greater and more honored in his kingdom than they had ever been before.

Now there are several things that this story teaches us.

I. The first is this: That *we ought to serve God, no matter what happens to us.*

These young men might have said, " There cannot be much harm in just bowing down to the ground and rising again, if it will save us from being burned to death."

But they knew that it was *wrong*, and conscience kept telling them, *God* says, "Thou shalt have no other gods before me." "Thou shalt not make unto thee any graven image." "Thou shalt not bow down to them nor worship them." And this was enough; and if they had a thousand lives to lose instead of one, they ought not to have disobeyed the commandment of God.

But I have seen people, and perhaps you have too, who were *afraid to do what was right*, for fear that they might suffer for it. Not that there was any danger of their being thrown into the fiery furnace, but then somebody would laugh at them, or be angry with them; and all the time they do not seem to remember that "*God* is angry with the wicked every day," and that it is very far better to please God than man.

Among the soldiers who have lately gone out from the city of Chicago, was a drummer boy only thirteen years old, who was

also a Sunday scholar. One day when they
were marching through the streets, the Captain saw a very beautiful flag flying over a
drinking-saloon, and he ordered his men to
halt and give it a salute. The boy
had always obeyed orders; but this time
he thought the salute was meant for the
place as well as for the flag, and he stood
still, and not a single beat was heard from
his drum. The Captain asked him the reason of this. "Sir," said the brave boy, "I
would not go into such a place as that, and
I cannot salute it." "My good boy," replied
the Captain, patting him on the shoulder,
"you are right and I am wrong." Now that
boy might have lost his place for trying to
do right, or some of the soldiers might
have laughed at him; but it made no dif-
ference; he felt that *God* smiled upon him,
and what more can any one want than
this?

He was like another little boy in Turkey,

who had in some way got a New Testament, which he had learned to read, and who had found his way to the Protestant chapel, where he loved to go and hear the missionary preach about Jesus Christ. But his father was very angry with him, and turned him out of his house, and told all his friends not to give him any work; so that the poor boy was without a home, and had no way of earning any money to support himself. His father told him that he would give him a great many things; yes, everything he wanted, if he would give up the Bible; but, although he obeyed his father in everything else, he could not do so in this, and all his answer was, " Christ has said, ' He that loveth father or mother more than me, is not worthy of me.' "

He *dared to do right*, no matter what might happen. He had made up his mind to *serve God*, even if he had to beg his bread from door to door, and sleep under the open sky. And I would say to every one of you. Do what is *right ; obey God*— obey this gospel of Christ, even if it seems ever so hard. Listen always to that voice of *conscience* in your heart, and though your companions laugh at you for trying to please God, and say many hard things about you because you will not do wrong with them, still, never mind : you will be happier than they can be, and *God* will love you, and take care of you.

II. A second lesson that we may learn from our text is : That *religion makes us brave.*

Did you ever hear of a braver thing than those three young men marching right up to the mouth of the furnace of fire, and letting the men throw them into it, when they might have saved their lives by bending their knees to the golden image ? Now it was *religion* that took away their fears. It

was their love to God, and their fear of sinning against Him, that made them so brave.
It was this that took away all *Daniel's* fear,
when they threw him into the den of lions.
It was this that made *Stephen* so calm and
happy when they were stoning him to death.
And it has made many a child brave enough
to *say no* when Satan tempted him to do
wrong, and helped him to obey God and to
obey his parents.

I have seen boys, and men too, who had
a very foolish way of thinking that they
were brave and manly when they were not
afraid to do wrong—to swear, to drink, to
break the Sabbath, or disobey any other of
God's commands. But I have sometimes
thought that those who do such things are
great cowards after all ; for the fact is, there
is something they are afraid of, and that is
to *do right*.   And is it not better and more
manly to fear wickedness than to fear goodness ? to fear God than to fear man ?

Let me tell you a little story that will show what I mean by being brave. There was a good boy who went off to sea in a great ship. Just before he went away from home his mother said to him, " *Never touch a drop of rum !*" Well, the other sailors drank their rum every day, and when it stormed they drank all the more, because they thought it would keep them from taking cold ; and they offered it to the boy, but he always said *no !* One day it stormed very hard, and they were all very wet, and they told him to take a little, or else he might become sick and die, and still the brave boy had courage to say *no !* But presently one of the sailors said he knew *he* could make him take a dram, so he tried very hard to do so, but he would not touch a drop : and then that boy told the old sailor of his mother's words—"Never drink a drop of rum"—and he repeated to him a great many texts of Scripture to show that his mother was

right—(for he had been a good Sunday-school scholar). The sailor had never heard so much Bible in his life as that little fellow poured into his ear, and all he could say was, " Your mother never stood watch on deck." But he gave up his task, and when the other sailors asked how he had succeeded, he said, " Oh, you can't do anything with him *he is so chuck full of the Bible.*"

Now that I should call a *brave boy.* He knew he was right, and God knew it too, and God helped him to say *no,* and to keep saying it as often as they tried to make him do wrong. A very little word that is, but how few are brave enough to say it! I hope you will all learn well that word, for you will often have need to use it. They who belong to the " Sunday-school army" ought to be such heroes that when any of them are asked to do wrong, they will say NO—if it costs them their life.

About fifteen hundred years ago, when
11

Christians were treated very cruelly, and so many of them were killed because they would not give up their Saviour, there was a Christian man at Antioch whom they were slowly murdering, telling him all the time that he must worship their gods, or else they would tear his flesh from his bones. At last, after answering their questions a great many times, he told the judge that any little child must see that it is better to worship one God, the Maker of the heaven and the earth, and one Saviour, who is able to bring us to God, than to worship the many idols of the heathen. Now when he said this, the judge saw a little boy eight or nine years old standing near by with his mother, and he pointed to the boy and told the Christian to put the question to him. He did so, and instantly the little boy answered, " God is one, and Jesus Christ is one with the Father." The wicked man then became very angry, and said, " This is a snare—you have told the child to come here and give that answer;" and then turning to the boy he asked, "How did you learn this?" The boy looked up to his mother's face and answered, "It was God's grace that taught it to my dear mother, and when I sat upon her knee, a baby, she taught me that Jesus loved little children, and I learned to love Him for His love to us."

"Let us see *now* what the love of Christ can do for you," said the cruel judge, and immediately his servants seized him and beat him with their sharp rods till the blood streamed out. "What can the love of Christ do for him now?" asked the judge. "It enables him to endure what his Master endured for him and for all of us," answered the mother.

And then they beat the child harder than before, and he asked, "What can the love of Christ do *now?*" And tears fell even from heathen eyes as the poor mother, who must have suffered a thousand times more than her poor boy, answered, "It teaches him to forgive his persecutors."

And the boy watched his mother's eye as it rose towards heaven for him, and he thought of the sufferings of his dear Lord and Saviour, and when they asked him whether he would deny Christ and serve their false gods, he answered, " *No*—there is no other God but one, and Jesus Christ is the Redeemer of the world. He loved me, and I love Him for His love."

Then the poor child fainted under their blows, and they threw the little suffering body into his mother's arms, and said, " See what the love of Christ can do for him *now.*" And the mother pressed him gently to her bleeding heart and answered, " That love will take him from the wrath of man to the peace of heaven," and so the poor boy died.

Now, was he not brave ? and what made him so ? Nothing but *religion*—nothing but the *grace of God* in his heart. And what

the love of Christ did for him it can do for
you and me. We may not have to become
martyrs for Christ, and to *die* for Him, but
we must all *live* for him, and if we love Him
and pray to Him, He will make us so strong
and brave that Satan cannot frighten us into
doing wrong. You may think that there is
no chance for doing *great things*, but the boy
or girl who tries hard every day to *do right
in little things*—to be kind, loving, patient,
forgiving,—to speak no angry words—to do
good to everybody, and always obey God—
such an one I call *a hero ;* and if you will
all give your hearts to God, as the three
children in Babylon did, then God will *help*
you as He helped them. He will take care
of you, and although you may not see any
bright angel walking with you among the
flames, or among the troubles by which Satan
or wicked people try to frighten you, still
His angel will be with you, for what says
the Bible : " The angel of the Lord encamp-

eth round about them that fear Him to deliver them." And that angel will go with
you as long as you live ; and what is still better, God's *Holy Spirit* will go with you. Then
you will not be afraid of any *troubles*, for
God's loving hand will wipe away your tears,
and comfort your heart when it aches and
grieves. You will not be afraid of any *duty*,
for if you love God it will be harder to do
wrong than to do right. You will not be
afraid to *die*, for Christ's lambs and Christ's
sheep can say to their shepherd when they go
to the dark valley, " *I will fear no evil, for
Thou art with me.*" You will not be afraid
when " the dead, small and great, shall stand
before God " at the dreadful *Judgment* day,
but will be able to say, " Christ died for
me ;" and then, instead of going with the
wicked to that lake of fire, which is a great
deal worse than the furnace in Babylon, you
will go to live with God and with the blessed angels in glory.

All this religion can do for you, if you will only give up your hearts to God.

And remember this, those three brave young men I have been telling you of, loved and served God *when they were little children*. You may do the same, and oh, you will never have a better time to do it than *now*. I pray God that he may help you to begin *to-day!*

VI.

The Child-Prophet.

"Children, hark! the Saviour's speaking
　　To you now:
Laborers in my vineyard wanting—
　　Who will go?

"Who will say, as once did Samuel,
　　Here am I,
Waiting, Lord, to do Thy pleasure
　　Till I die?

"Who will give their all to Jesus,
　　And receive
Of His grace a tenfold measure
　　While they live?

"And when earthly toil is ended
　　Here below,
Wear a fadeless crown of glory;
　　Who will go?"

The Child-Prophet.

THERE is hardly any greater blessing in this world than to have a *pious mother ;* a mother who loves the Saviour, and tries to make her children love Him too ; a mother who prays for us, and prays with us, and leads us kindly to the Lord Jesus, that He may take away our sins. A child or youth may have ever so beautiful a house, and his parents may be rich, and able to gratify all his desires, but if he has not a pious, praying *mother*, he is not half so well off as many a poor child whom I could name to you.

I can remember a great many things that have happened since I was a little boy ;

but there is nothing that I remember more plainly than the soft, low voice of my mother, (who is now in heaven,) as she used to kneel by my bedside when I had gone to rest, and pray that her child might grow up to love and serve the Saviour. I seem to hear that voice now, and I shall never forget it as long as this heart beats.

Oh, thank God for giving to so many of you this rich blessing! You do not know its value now—but you *will* know it when that kind voice is hushed, and that loving heart is stilled in death. Then you will wish, if you do not before, that you had obeyed her kind counsels, and followed her good example.

Now, *Samuel* was blessed with such a mother. Her name was *Hannah*, and when he was but a babe, she brought him up to the house of God and gave him to the Lord, saying, " I have lent him to the Lord ; as long as he liveth, he shall be lent to the

Lord." And God heard that mother's prayers, and took the child, and, young as he was, let him remain in His house with Eli, who was then the high priest. We do not know exactly what he did, but we read that he " ministered to the Lord," by which, I suppose, it is meant that he helped Eli about the altar. And he did his work so well that Eli permitted him to wear a little linen ephod, just like the older priests. It must have been a beautiful sight—a little boy serving God in His house, and helping to offer the sacrifices, and burn the sweet incense, with which the church in those days worshipped God. In these delightful duties he grew older and larger, and, the Bible tells us, was " in favor with God and man."

He was probably about twelve years old when, one night, after he had lain down to sleep in his little bed, which was near to Eli's room, (so that he could hear him, if he should call,) he heard a voice, saying, " *Samuel, Samuel.*" Thinking it was the high priest who called, he ran to him, and said, " Here am I ; for thou calledst me." But Eli said, " I called not—lie down again ;" and he went and lay down. Then he heard the voice once more, and again ran to Eli, but received the same answer, and returned to his bed again, not knowing what to make of it. But the voice did not stop, and so a *third* time he stood before Eli, and said, " Here am I, for thou *didst* call me." And then Eli saw that the Lord had called the child, and he told him to lie down again, and if he heard the voice, to say, " Speak Lord, for thy servant heareth."

" *Samuel, Samuel,*" once more, said that strange voice, and when the child heard it, he said, " Speak, Lord, for thy servant heareth !" And then God spoke to him, and told him how wicked the sons of Eli had been, and how their father had not re-

strained or punished them, and told him
how He would Himself punish them, and
never forgive their great sin.

When morning came, Samuel said nothing of what the Lord had told him, but
went and opened the doors of God's house
as usual. Then Eli told him that he must
not hide from him what God had said ; and
so he told him all. And very soon it was
all fulfilled : for Eli's wicked sons were
killed in a battle ; and Eli himself, when
he heard of it, and was told that the ark of
God had been taken by their enemies, fell
back in his chair and died.

Thus Samuel, when but a small boy, became a prophet of the Lord ; and when he
grew up, he became one of the greatest
prophets that ever lived. I should like to
tell you more of his history, but I hope you
will read it for yourselves in the Bible.

Now, there are several things that this
story of Samuel teaches us.

I. The first is this : that *it is a very happy thing for children to be given up by their parents to the Lord, as Samuel was.*

A few years ago, a father and a mother stood in the house of God, before the pulpit, with a little babe in their arms. The minister solemnly addressed them, before the whole congregation, and prayed earnestly and tenderly for that little one, that it might be made one of the lambs of the Saviour's flock ; and oh, how many hearts prayed with him ! Then those parents promised, before God, and angels, and men, that they would bring up that child to love and serve God ; and the minister sprinkled it with water, in the name of the Father, and the Son, and the Holy Ghost. A few short years rolled on. God spared that child's life, and it grew, and began to attend the Sabbath-school, and learn the way to heaven. He cannot, perhaps, remember the day when he was thus given to God ; but his parents remember it, and God remembers it, and I wish now to remind you of it—for it is of *you*, my dear young friend, that I am speaking—*you are that child.* For, many of you have been given to God just as Samuel was; and the *hearts* of your pious father and mother said, when the water of baptism was sprinkled upon you, "I have lent him to the Lord, as long as he liveth, he shall be lent to the Lord."

Do you ever think *what was meant* by your being given to God before all the people? I will tell you. You were given to Him *to be saved by Him*, and *to be used by Him.*

First, *to be saved by Him*, because you are a sinner, and have a wicked heart, and can never go to heaven unless your sins are blotted out in the blood of Christ, and your heart is changed for a new one that will love and serve the Saviour. But do not think that your being baptized will save

12*

you, or that your father's or mother's prayers will save you, unless you *yourself* repent
of sin and believe on the Lord Jesus Christ.
God loves the dear lambs of His flock, and
Jesus loves them, oh how tenderly, and has
died for them, and wants you all to become
His children ; but you cannot become such
unless you give *yourselves*—your hearts—
your all—away to Jesus, who now says to
you, " My son, my daughter, *give me thy
heart.*"

And then you were given to God, as
Samuel was, *to be used by Him.* Do you
not think God has *a right* to use you just as
He pleases ?   He who made these hands
and feet, shall He not employ them in His
service ?   He who gave us these voices,
shall He not hear them in daily prayer and
praise ?   He who gave us these thinking
minds, and these warm, loving hearts, can
He not claim them as His own ?   Oh, you
belong to God more than you belong to

your parents, yes and more than you belong
to *yourselves*. And when you think of the
hand that made you and preserves you;
when you think of your having been solemnly given back to your Creator, ought you
not to feel, "*I am the Lord's*"? And what
then? Why, if "I am the Lord's," then I must
serve Him and obey His will, and minister
unto Him as Samuel did. I must be holy,
and be as much as I can like the angels
who "serve Him day and night in His
temple."

And here let me say that if you

"Want to be an angel, and with the angels stand,
  A crown upon your forehead, a harp within your
    hand,"

as you so often sing, in that beautiful hymn,
then you must *do as the angels do*—that is,
live for God, and not for yourselves, and
serve Him with all your powers.

II. For, another thing that the story of

Samuel teaches us is, *that the youngest children may serve God.*

But, I hear some one asking, " Can we live, as he did, in God's house, and minister at the altar, in a little linen ephod? and can we hear God calling to us as He called the little prophet? Oh, if we could, how quickly we should answer, ' Speak, Lord, for thy servant heareth!'"

Would you answer the voice of God so quickly if it called aloud to you? Well, let me tell you that although He does not now call young children to do the work of His house as He did Samuel, He yet speaks *this very moment*, and speaks at all times to every one of you. He calls every child and youth—(yes, and every grown person too)—calls you by His holy *Word*, and calls by His *Spirit* in your hearts. Listen—do you not hear Him : " My son, give me thy heart ;" " Remember now thy Creator in the days of thy youth ;" " They that seek

me early shall find me." Whose voice is
that? Ah! it is the voice of *God*, and
these, *these* are His calls to every one of
you. Oh, that you could not only hear, but
obey them!

God calls you, then, to serve Him; and
in what ways are you to do this? I have
said that you were given to God to be
saved by Him, and so the first thing you
must do is to "*believe on the Lord Jesus
Christ:*" to take Him as *your* Saviour, and
love Him with all your heart. God commands you to do this, and you cannot be
saved in any other way.

Is it a *hard thing* to love Christ when
He has so loved you, and has laid down
His life for you? Surely, it should not be
hard!

There was once a poor man who worked
in one of the mines in England, who had an
only and loving son. Every day when he
went down into the mines to work, he would

take his boy with him, and when night came, they were both drawn up again by a rope and bucket, and returned to their happy home. One evening, when they were being drawn up together in this way, the father heard a cracking noise above him. He looked up, and saw that *the rope was breaking*, and that only three or four strands of it were left to hold him and his darling child from destruction. What was to be done? The rope was not strong enough to bring them both to the top, and so one or both of them must perish. The father loved life, but he loved his child more; and so, leaving his boy in the bucket, he said, "There, my child, lie quiet for a few moments, and you will be safe at the top," and then threw himself over and was dashed to pieces. How very great was the love of that father for his son! But greater still is the love of Christ for your soul, for He has given *His* life to save you; and if you only trust

Him and obey Him, you will be brought safely up, not by a broken rope, but by a mighty, everlasting arm to His glorious home.

Now Christ says, " I love them that love me ;" and no child that knows who Christ is, is too young to love Him and be saved by Him.

Another way in which you may serve God is by *doing good*. See the youthful Samuel, assisting with his little hands the aged Eli in the house of God. So you may, every one of you, help your pastor, and help the church, in our work of doing good, and saving souls from death. Who of you, for instance, cannot set a good example to those around you? who cannot speak kind words for Christ and His Church? who cannot give something to send the Bible to the heathen? who cannot bring at least a few poor, neglected boys or girls into the Sabbath-school, that they may be pointed to heaven? Oh, there are ways enough if one only has a mind to improve them. There is work for the smallest hands, work for the youngest hearts, and if you have the *piety* of Samuel, you may be as *useful* and as *happy* as he was. Why, there are children and youths now living, who have done more for Christ already, than some of the gray-haired members of the churches. Jesus was not more than twelve years old when He began to go about doing good, and said, " Wist ye not that I must be about my Father's business?" This shows that all who have reached that age are old enough to be about that business — serving and obeying God.

A little girl who loved the Saviour, tried to follow His example of going about and doing good; and many were the hearts that she cheered by her kind words and deeds, and her sunny smile—(for there are many,

many times where a smile will be a rich blessing to those around us.) But God called her, when she was ten years old, to serve Him with the angels in glory. When they told her she was going to die, she .looked up to her father, who loved her dearly, and did not know how to part with her, and said, "Dear papa, how much do I cost you every year?"

He thought the child was getting out of her mind, when she asked such a question; but he answered, to soothe her, "Well, dearest, perhaps two hundred dollars. What then, darling?"

"Because," said she, "I thought, may be you would lay it out this year in Bibles, for poor children, to, remember me by."

"Yes, I will, my precious child," said the father, "I will do it every year as long as I live, and thus my Lilian shall yet speak, and draw hundreds and thousands after her to heaven."

13

She loved nothing so much as to serve God; and even when she lay in pain and feebleness on her dying-bed, she forgot herself and her sufferings in the one thought, how she might do good to others, and glorify her Maker.

This is the spirit that we want you all to have, who have been given to God as Lilian was, and as Samuel was, *to be used by Him.*

III. And there is one other thing taught in the story of Samuel, that I shall not have time to say much about, but I will just mention it: it is that *God loves and honors early piety.*

See the child Samuel made a prophet of the Lord, ministering in God's house, and God talking with him in the night, just as friend talks with friend; and then see him growing up to be one of the best, and greatest, and most useful men that ever lived.

Now, this was because he *did not put off serving God* until he was a man, as so many do, but gave his heart right up to Him as soon as he knew who God was.

So you, my dear children, if you will now do as Samuel did, may be as happy and as honored as he was ; may hear God talking with your soul ; may enjoy His loving presence, and grow up to be useful and respected. You may not indeed be prophets, but I hope some of you will be *ministers*, and be great blessings to the church and the world by preaching the gospel, and saving souls from . death.

And God not only honors *the lives* of those who serve him in their early years, but honors them *in death*, by bestowing His grace upon them, and giving them a heaven-like happiness.

Thus died a little Italian girl, whose name was Carlotta. As two merchants, one of whom was an infidel, were one day

leaving an eating-house in one of our cities,
a strain of soft music came through an open
door, and it was so marvellously sweet that
they followed the child who was singing it,
and asked her to sing some more for them.
She was very poor, and was wrapped up in
a patched cloak and a patched hood, and
her little shoes were full of holes : but her
father, who was an organ-grinder, was sick,
and she had come out to beg some money to
keep them from starving.

Her first song was that beautiful one,—

> " There is a happy land,
> Far, far away."

When she had finished it, the infidel said
to her, " Where did you learn that song ?"

" In Sabbath-school, sir," was her answer.

" And you don't suppose there is a happy
land, do you ?" asked the man, who tried
not to believe in heaven or hell.

" *I know there is*," said she, quietly and

decidedly, "and I'm going to sing there. My mother said so. She used to sing to me until she was sick, then she said she wasn't going to sing any more on earth, but up in heaven."

The two men pitied the poor little girl, and followed her home, and gave her some shoes and some money, and promised to go and see her again. About a month afterwards they went together to the gloomy home of the organ-grinder and found that he was dead, and that little Carlotta was very sick.

"I wish I could sing for you," said she, "but it hurts me. It won't hurt me up there, will it?" They asked her if she had heard of Jesus. "Yes," said she, "*good Jesus;*" and when the m'n began to weep, she said, "Don't cry—don't cry ; *I can't cry—I'm so glad.* Glad to get away from here. I used to be so cold in the long winters, for we didn't have fire sometimes, but
13*

mother used to hug me close, and sing about heaven, and tell me if I was His, the Saviour would love me and give me a better home ; and so I gave myself to Him, and oh, I shall *sing* there, and be *so happy !* Christ sent a little angel in my dream— mother told me He would, and that angels would carry me up there." Then she was still for a little while ; but presently the hands moved—the arms were raised—the eyes opened and turned upward. " See, see," she cried, " oh, there is mother, and there are the angels, and they are *all singing—all singing.*" Her voice faltered— her arms fell—but a heavenly brightness lingered on her face ; and they knew that her spirit had gone to join her mother and the angels.

Can you wonder that even the strong infidel was melted before such a scene ? He had resisted everything else—men had talked and pleaded with him in vain—but there, by the bedside of the little child, his hard heart was softened, and he knelt down with his friend, and prayed that he, too, might have the same faith and hope that had enabled Carlotta to die in such happy triumph.

Oh, my dear young friends, may this faith and hope *be yours*—that you, too, may say, " I'm going to sing in heaven!" May the God of Samuel be your God! may his holy, blessed childhood and youth be yours! and yours his heavenly home!

VII.

The Treasure-Finders.

"Go thou in life's fair morning,
   Go in the bloom of youth,
And dig for thine adorning
   The precious pearl of truth:
Secure this heavenly treasure
   And bind it on thy heart,
And let no earthly pleasure
   E'er cause it to depart.

"Go while the day-star shineth,
   Go while thy heart is light;
Go e'er thy strength declineth,
   While every sense is bright:
Sell all thou hast, and buy it,
   'Tis worth all earthly things—
Rubies, and gold, and diamonds,
   Sceptres and crowns of Kings."

The Treasure-Finders.

"I love them that love me, and they that seek me early shall find me."—Prov viii. 17.

DO you know what it is that is worth more than choice silver and fine gold, that is better than diamonds and rubies, and all kinds of costly gems—and so very precious, that "all the things that may be desired are not to be compared to it?"

It must be some *very great treasure*, you will say, if it is more valuable than anything else that we could wish for.

And so it is? Suppose that all the mountains that are in the world were made of gold—they could not buy it, or make us half as *rich* as this can. Or, suppose that you had all the pleasures that there are in the whole world, they could not make you half so *happy* as this can make you. And yet, precious, lovely, costly as it is—it is offered to you all "without money and without price."

"*What is it?—what is it?*" I think I hear you ask. If you will open your Bibles and read the eighth chapter of the Book of Proverbs, you will there learn all about it.

In that chapter it is called "*wisdom;*" but I think you will not read it all through without seeing that this is only another name for *a person* who speaks to us so often in God's word—*Jesus Christ.*

Now, see how *earnest* Christ is. In the first three verses, He says that He "standeth in the top of the high places, by the way, in the places of the paths;" "crieth at the gates, at the entrance of the city"—that is, *everywhere*, where there are people to listen to Him. And what does He say? "Unto you, O men, I call, and my voice is to the sons of men." But he does not stop with calling

men and women—He also says : " *Hearken
unto me. oh ye children*, for blessed are they
that keep my ways." Do you ask, why are
they blessed? The last two verses answer
the question, and show us the reason of
our Saviour's loud, earnest call—" For who-
so findeth me findeth life, and shall obtain favor of the Lord ; but he that sinneth against
me wrongeth his own soul : *all they that
hate me love death.*" And in the seventeenth
verse He says—(and I want you to think as
you read it, that these are the words of the
kind *Jesus*, who once took little children in
His arms and blessed them)—" I love them
that love me, and *they that seek me early
shall find me.*"

Now, I wish to show you three things :

I. *Why* you ought to seek Christ ;

II. *How* you must seek him ; and

III. Why you ought to *seek Him early :*
that is, while you are young.

14

I. I suppose I need not take much time to tell you *why* you ought to seek Him, for every Sabbath scholar knows that we cannot be happy in this world or the next without Jesus Christ. But I am so anxious that you should all give your hearts to the Saviour *now*, that I will try to give you some reasons why you should do it.

One of these reasons is contained in those sweet words of Jesus, "*I love them that love me.*" Is it not a pleasant thing to be *loved* by our parents and friends? How unhappy we should be if nobody loved us or cared for us! But what a delightful thing it must be to know that *Jesus Christ* loves us —Christ, the Son of God—Christ, the great King of Heaven and earth; who is so *powerful* that He is able to give us all that we need for the body or the soul; Christ, who is so *good*, that He is always making His friends happy, and answering their prayers, and refusing them nothing that is good for them;

Christ, who is so *true*, that He never prom-
ises anything that he will not perform;
Christ, the *friend of sinners*, who gave Himself—*His own life*—that, with His blood,
He might wash away our sins; and who
opens for us the pearly gates of heaven,
that we may enter and be forever happy!
Oh, to be loved by Christ is to have the
best friend, the sweetest pleasures, the
greatest riches, the surest hopes, and the
brightest glories that can be found in earth
or heaven! And should you not seek Him
as *your* friend, *your* Saviour, when He can
become all this *to you?* Should you not
love Him with all your hearts, when he
so loves you that He has given *Himself* for
you?

I wish that every child and youth could
love Him as a little girl of six years
did, who died a few years ago. When
they told her that she was dying, she asked
her sister to read to her from the Bible

about Christ's blessing little children ; and
then she said, " How kind ! I shall soon go
to Jesus ; He will soon take *me* up in His
arms, and bless *me, too*, and no disciple shall
keep me away." Her sister kissed her, and
said, " Do you love me ? "   " Yes, my dear,"
she replied ; " but do not be angry if *I love
Jesus better*."

Another reason why you should seek
Christ is, that *you are sinners*, and Christ
takes the wicked heart and washes out all
its stains, and makes it " whiter than snow."
You must have your sins forgiven, or you can
never wear a crown in Heaven, and *none but
Christ* can forgive them. And He can give you
a heart to love and serve Him in this world,
and to praise Him forever in the place which
He has prepared for them that love **Him**.

II. But I hear some one asking, " *How
shall* I seek Him ? Jesus Christ is away up
in Heaven, and I am on the earth ; if I seek

Him ever so hard, how do I know that I can find Him?"

A lady and gentleman who were travelling, one evening lost their way. Coming to a cross-road, they saw a guide-board. The gentleman got out; and though he could but just see, yet, by going close up to the board, he made out to find a direction which helped him to find his way to the place he wished to visit. Now, suppose he had refused to look at the board, and had gone on blundering in the dark, and had not found the place he sought all night—what would you have said of him? *Served him right.* Just so. A man who is lost, and refuses to look at a guide-board, deserves to wander a good while, as a punishment of his folly. But would not such conduct be just as foolish in boys and girls, and would not a long tramp in the dark be a just punishment for them, too? I think that it would.

Now, you need not go long in the dark to
14*

seek Christ. *The Bible* is your guide-
board. It tells you which way to go ; it
warns you against by-paths and wrong
roads, against false guides, and pits and
traps, and other dangers. And it is not only
a *guide-board*, but a *companion* all the way,
if you will only keep by its side ; and not
only a companion, but a *lamp* to your feet
and a light to your path. Though it be
ever so dark all around you, it will lead you
straight to this Friend whom you seek—
straight to the Saviour. And more than
this, Jesus Himself will *help you* to find
Him, by putting His Holy Spirit in your
hearts. He will meet you more than half-
way ; and while you are all trembling and
anxious, lest you do not reach Him, all at
once you will hear His voice of welcome in
your hearts, and feel yourself taken in the
arms and carried in the bosom of the kind
Shepherd.

Now look with me at this guide-board,

and let us try to read its directions. What does it say to us? "*Except ye* REPENT, *ye shall all likewise perish.*" Here, then, is the first step towards the Saviour. It looks like a narrow, thorny path, but if it leads to Christ it is, after all, pleasant. There are not many travelling it, but we can see that those who are in it are Christ's people, while the crowds in yonder broad road are His enemies ; and who had not rather go in a narrow road to heaven than in a broad one to hell? So let us enter this narrow path. You will see as you enter it, that every one, like Christian in the "Pilgrim's Progress," has his *burden*. That is, all who repent feel weighed down under a sense of sin. Do you, my dear young friend, feel this burden? Do you feel a sorrow for your sin and naughtiness? If you do not you are in the *wrong path*, and I fear you will be lost. Oh, think, then, of that wicked heart of yours, and confess its wickedness to Jesus, and then the burden will roll off at His cross. For see, He stands in the narrow way, and says, " Come unto me, all ye that labor and are heavy laden, and I will give you rest.

But look again at the guide-board. What is this that we see ? "BELIEVE *on the Lord Jesus Christ and thou shalt be saved.*" A little child once woke up in the night and found that the house was on fire. He was away up stairs, and his father slept below, and he saw that the stairs were all in flames, and he could not get down. What should he do ? He ran to the window, and there he heard *his father's* voice, though he could not *see* him in the crowd, and the father said, " *Jump, my child, and I will catch you.*" The little boy trembled, for it was a long leap for him to take, and he feared it might kill him. But the hot fire was all around him, and he knew that he would be burned to death if he stayed where he was. He clung to the window, looked at the flames, heard his father shouting to him to let go, thought of that father's strong arms and loving heart, and then *let go his hold,* and in an instant found himself, unhurt, in his father's arms.

Now, that boy had *faith* in his parent's promise, in his strength and in his love. So you, dear children, who are in this world that is to be burned up, and who are all the time drawing nearer and nearer to the dreadful fire of God's wrath hereafter, do you not hear the Saviour's voice, saying; " Flee from the wrath to come ?" And as you ask, *How* shall I flee, Christ says, " *Let yourself drop into my strong arms.*" Oh, take Jesus at his word ! *Trust Him ;* as your Saviour, let go of everything else, of every other hope, of every thought of your own goodness, and fall into His arms, and then you will have come to Christ, and found Him as your Saviour.

Does some one say, " I want to repent and

believe, and I try to do so, but I do not find Jesus yet?" Let us look at the guide-board again, and see if it has anything to meet *your* case. I read on it these words: " STRIVE *to enter in at the straight gate.*" Here, then, is another kind direction.

Now, if it were a *million dollars* that you were seeking, do you not think that you would try pretty hard before you gave it up? If you were *drowning*, would you not struggle with all your might to keep your head above water and reach the shore? But Christ is worth more to you than all the gold in the world, and you ought to struggle much harder to save your perishing soul than your dying body. Christ wants you *to be in earnest* when you seek Him, for oh, He was in earnest when He left His glorious home, and came down to suffer and die upon the cross that such as you might come to Him and be saved.

I wish you were as earnest in seeking

Christ as six poor little boys near Philadel-
phia were a few winters ago. They used to
meet every evening in the open air, and in the
coldest weather, under a large oak tree, for
prayer, until at last a pouring rain drove them
to seek shelter in the office of a good man,
who told them they could meet there as often
as they chose to do so. Think of it! Not
even the winter's cold and storm could keep
them from the spot where they were seeking
Christ.

And this reminds me of another direction
that you will find on the guide-board, (for
you see it is very full and very plain,) "ASK
and ye shall receive." What delightful
words these are! Do you want repentance?
" Ask and ye shall receive!" Do you want
faith? "Ask and ye shall receive!" Do
you want your sins forgiven? your soul washed in the blood of Christ? Do you want
to be made holy? want happiness, want
heaven? Christ says to you, "*Ask and ye*

shall receive ! " In other words, "*Pray!* " Go right to Christ with all your wants and tell him how hard your heart is, and how you desire a new one ; how weak your faith is, and how you wish it strengthened ; how you want Christ to become your friend, and want strength and grace to serve Him, and Christ will hear your prayer, and while you seek you will find !

You need not do as a little boy did who wanted to pray and hardly knew how to do it. He used to write little notes to the Saviour, and throw them out of the window, hoping that Christ would find them. If you pray with the heart, your prayers will rise, quicker than lightning, to the throne of Jesus—and so quickly does he hear prayer that He has said of his people, " *Before they call I will answer, and while they are yet speaking I will hear !* "

This, then, is the way you must come to Jesus—do not forget it—with *repentance,*

with *faith*, with *earnestness*, and with *prayer*. And if you come in this way you will surely find Him ; for he says to us, " Him that cometh unto me I will in no wise cast out." " *Every one* that asketh receiveth, and *every one* that seeketh findeth."

Will you not come to the Saviour?

III. " Yes," some child or youth replies, " *I will come* when I am *a little older !* " But does the smallest child think that he is *too young* to seek Christ? If so, you make a great mistake. There is one little word in my text that has a great deal of meaning, and I must now, in the third place, say a few words about it ; the word " *early*," " They that seek me *early* shall find me."

A Sabbath-school teacher lately asked her class the question, " How soon ought a child to give its heart to God ? " One little girl answered, " When thirteen years old," another, " *ten ;*" another " *six*." At length the
15

last and smallest child in the class answered,
' *Just as soon as we know who God is.*"

That child *was right*. No doubt she had
read in the Bible those beautiful words,
" Suffer *the little children* to come unto me."
Now, is there a child who reads or hears
these words who does not know who God
is? I think not. Well, if you know who
God and Christ are, and know what it is to
be sorry for sin, and to love and trust the
Lord Jesus, then you are old enough to seek
Christ, and it is high time for you to give
your hearts to Him.

There are a great many reasons why you
should do this, and no reason at all why you
should not do it.

(1.) Do you think you are *too young to be
happy?* No, you say, happiness is just the
thing we want. Well, then you are not too
young to *seek Christ*, for, as I have tried to
show you, Christ alone can make you happy.

His "ways are ways of pleasantness," and
all his "paths are peace." I have known
young people who said they would not become Christians yet, because they wished to
be happy a few years longer. Why, they
know nothing about religion, if they think
they can be half as happy without it as they
can be with it.

"How long have you been a Christian?"
said one old man to another. "Fifty years,"
said he. "Well," asked the other, "have you
ever been sorry that you began so young to
serve the Saviour?" "Oh, no," said the old
man, and the tears trickled down his furrowed
cheeks, "I weep when I think of the sins of
my youth! It is this that makes me weep
now!"

An aged woman who had been a Christian
for more than fifty years, lay on her dying
bed. She said, "Tell all the children that
an old woman who is just on the borders of
eternity, is very much grieved that she did

not begin to love Christ *when a child.* Tell them *youth* is the time to serve the Lord.

And so there are a great many who are grieved that they did not serve Christ earlier —but I never heard of a Christian being sorry that he had served him when a child; and this proves that the sooner you seek Jesus the happier you will be.

(2.) Another reason is, that it is *a great deal easier* for you to seek Him now than it will be by-and-by.

A few years ago two men were floating in a little boat on the Niagara river, both fast asleep. Soon the boat began to move slowly along towards the falls. They might then have been saved, but they slept on, and did not dream of their danger. When they awoke they were in the rapids. They seized the oars and worked with all the power of their strong arms, but it did no good—*it was too late.* One of them was dashed over the falls in an instant : the other, after holding on to a log of wood for twenty hours, was also carried over the dreadful falls, and killed. Do you not think that poor man, in those twenty hours of hopeless life, looked back and wished that he had *awoke a little earlier*, before the stream had floated him quite so far?

My young friend the stream of sin is like that river. It grows stronger and faster every moment, and the Lord Jesus knows well how hard it will be for you to escape by-and-by. So He stands on the shore and calls you to take hold of the rope of salvation that He throws out to you, and says, "They that seek me *early*, shall find me." "*Now* is the accepted time, behold *now* is the day of salvation."

Does repentance seem hard to you to-day? It will be harder yet *to-morrow* Does it seem hard to give up your hearts to Jesus now? It will be harder still the next time that He calls you.

15*

The *next time*, do I say? But who knows whether He will call you again? An old Jewish Rabbi once said to his disciples, "Turn to God *one* day before you die." "But how can a man know the day of his death?" asked one of them. He answered, "Therefore you should turn to God *to-day*, for perhaps you may die *to-morrow*, and so *every* day will be spent in turning to Him." Here then, is *another* reason for seeking Christ early, that if you wait much longer you may have *no chance* to seek Him. Your hearts may cease to beat before you have given them to God—your hands may be cold and still before they have engaged in Christ's service—and your voice silent in death, before it has prayed, " God be merciful to me a sinner.

I always love to close with *a promise*, and here I have one that belongs to little children, and to all who are young; and it comes from the Lord Jesus himself, and so we know that it is true—" They that seek me *early, shall find me.*" You may seek for *riches* and be disappointed; for *pleasures* and they will fly from you; for *long life,* and be brought to an early grave; but if you seek earnestly for *Christ,* He will not hide Himself from you, for they that seek Him early "*shall find Him.*" And when you find Jesus, you will find the " pearl of great price,"—will find peace, joy, happiness treasures in heaven—will find a golden crown hereafter, and a glorious home where Christ is!

Oh, forget not these sweet words of Jesus, but think of them day and night, " I love them that love me, and they that seek me early shall find me." And as you hear Christ whispering them to your hearts, will you not try to say, as David did, " *Thy face Lord will I seek!*" and pray with David, "Oh, satisfy me *early* with thy mercy, that I may rejoice and be glad all my days?"

VIII.

The Song of the Kingdom.

"CHILDREN of the Heavenly King,
  As ye journey, sweetly sing :
  Sing your Saviour's worthy praise,
  Glorious in His works and ways.

" Ye are travelling home to God
  In the way the fathers trod ;
  They are happy now, and ye
  Soon their happiness shall see.

" Shout, ye ' little flock,' and blest,
  You near Jesus' Throne shall rest .
  There your seats are now prepared,
  There your kingdom and reward."

The Song of the Kingdom.

· · · · 'The children crying in the temple, and saying, Hosanna to the Son of David." MATTHEW xxi. 15

PERHAPS there are some people who think that it is a new thing for the children to have their own little service in the church, and that there is nothing in the Bible about it. Now, I am going to show you that it is a very old thing. I am going to tell you about a children's service that was held by some Jewish boys and girls more than eighteen hundred years ago.

If you read the first eleven verses of this chapter, you will see that the Lord Jesus Christ had just rode into Jerusalem with a great many people going before Him and following Him, who were all very joyful, and who tried in every way to show their joy.

Some took off their coats and spread them over the road, as if the very ground was not good enough for Him to ride upon. Some cut down branches of the beautiful palm trees, and waved them in the air, and scattered them over the road, and all the time the great crowd—(Matthew says they were "a very great multitude,")—kept shouting and singing together, "*Hosanna to the Son of David. Blessed is He that cometh in the name of the Lord: Hosanna in the highest.*"

So they all came together into Jerusalem; and then Jesus went straight up to the temple, and there He saw a beautiful sight. A great many children had ran in there when they saw Christ coming: and I have no doubt they knew, when they looked upon His kind, gentle face, that he was the children's Friend. Perhaps some of them had been by when He took the little ones in His arms and blessed them. But, however that might have been, they began to sing that wonderful song, "*Hosanna to the Son of David*" and I have no doubt they sang it very sweetly.

Now the chief priests and Scribes, (the ministers who lived in those days), had never held any children's services, as we have, and they were very much surprised to hear their little voices in the house of God—as if they had not as good a right as any to praise their Saviour! And they frowned on them, and looked very angry, and said with their eyes, if not with their tongues, what business have you here, singing about Jesus? For they were wicked men, and hated Jesus with all their hearts. But they did not dare to stop them; and so they came to Christ, and said, with an ugly sneer, "Hearest Thou what these say?" And what did Jesus answer them? His answer was a beautiful one: "Have ye never read, Out of the mouths of babes and sucklings Thou hast perfected praise?" It was as if he had

16

said, " You ought to have known from what
David says in the Psalms about Christ, that
even little children may praise Him." And
so they sang away, till the walls of the old
temple rang again, and Jesus stood and
smiled on them, just as He smiles on you
from the skies when He sees you in His
house ; and that was *the first children's service.* Is it not a pleasant thought that the
first song to Jesus, in God's own house, when
He was upon earth, was sung by the lambs
of His flock ? I think he meant to show by
this that, while he wants us *all* to praise
Him, He takes great delight in the praises
of *youthful voices,* when he hears them singing the songs of His kingdom.

I. Now, the first thing I wish to say to
you about my text is this · that *children
should love the house of God.* They had often
been there with their parents, and looked
with solemn wonder upon the house where

God dwelt, and felt happy in worshipping Him.

So God wants that you *all* should love His church. Suppose you had a great and powerful friend living near by, who was all the time giving you many beautiful presents, and he should ask you to come often to his house, that he might give you more and better gifts : do you think you would stay away, and tell him, "I don't like your house, and don't want to go there? " Why no ; you would go just as often as you could, and would be very thankful that he let you come. Now God is all the time making you presents. He gives you life and health, and parents and friends, and home and food and clothing, and the Bible, and the Sabbath-school, and, the best of all, His own Son Jesus Christ, to save you from Hell and take you to Heaven. And the Church is *God's house*, where He lets His friends come and visit, and talk with Him, and where He

talks with them by His Word and His Holy
Spirit, and where he gives rich heavenly
gifts to their souls, and prepares them to go
to Heaven when they die. He has a great
many churches, but he lives in all of them.
Although you cannot see Him, He is in His
house whenever you go there, looking
straight into all your hearts, and wanting,
oh, how much, to do you good, and make
you happy as the angels, if you will only let
Him. And ought you not to *love* this house
of your best Friend, and to love His holy
day, and to love to pray and sing to Him?

I have seen children who think that Sunday is a very dull, stupid kind of a day, and
the church a dull sort of a place. But I
know why they think so—they do not love,
in their hearts, their best Friend. If they
did, I am sure they would love His house.

"Mamma," said a little girl, one day,
"don't you wish Sunday came right after
Wednesday? Sunday, Monday, Tuesday

Wednesday, and then *Sunday* again?"
" Why, my darling," answered her mother,
"God has arranged the week in His own
wise way, and I am sure it is the best, I
should not like it different." " But, mamma,"
said the little girl, " is it not so selfish in us
to keep for ourselves six days, while we give
only one to God? So selfish, mamma, and
He gives us everything we have!" Ah, she
loved God's day, and loved God's house, and
thought that she could not go there too
often.

And you ought to love it for another reason. You read in your Bibles about the
great gates of Heaven, that are made of
beautiful pearls, and you have often thought
how you would like to see them—they must
be so splendid. I hope you *will* all see them
when you die. But do you know that
Heaven has a great many gates in this world
that you can see with these eyes, and can go
through with these little feet? It is so ; for

what did Jacob say about the place where he worshipped God? "This is none other but the house of God, and *this is the gate of Heaven*." That is, God's house is one of the *outer gates* of that beautiful city; and when we come into it Heaven *seems nearer* than it does anywhere else. Here we learn about Heaven, and here God comes down to our souls and helps us to prepare for that happy land. Now, I know that you all want to go to Heaven. Will you not then, remember when the church-bell rings out its sweet Sabbath call, that it is all the time saying to you—" Come to the house of God—come to the gate of Heaven? Oh, I am sure that if you ask God to give you a new heart—a heart to love Him—you will love His house as those children did who went up to the temple to sing. Then you will love it as a dear little child in Wales did, about sixty years ago, of whom I want to tell you.

She used to walk a great ways to the

church, and the minister, when he met her
one day, stopped to talk with her a little ;
for she always listened so earnestly to his
preaching that he felt very much interested
in her ; and she was always able to tell him
the text he had preached from on the last
Sunday. But this time, when he asked her
for the text, she hung her head and could
not answer him. He asked again, and she
began to cry ; and then she said the weather
had been so bad that she could not get to
read the Bible. " Why, how was that ? "
said the minister. Then she told him that
there was no Bible at her home, or among
her friends, and so she had travelled every
week, on foot, *seven miles* to a place where
there was a Welsh Bible, on purpose to read
the chapter from which the minister had
taken his text ; but that week it had been
so cold and stormy that she could not go.

Now I wonder how many of these dear
children, with your Bibles in your houses

can tell your minister the next time he meets,
you what was the text of his last sermon,
and in what book, and chapter, and verse it
is to be found? Oh, *love* God's house, love
the preaching, the singing, the praying ; and
may the church be to you all a beautiful gate
of Heaven, until you shall have passed beyond it, and through the pearly gates on
high into the golden streets of the New
Jerusalem.

II. A second thing that our text teaches
is, that *children have reason to praise Christ.*
In the temple they sang, " Hosanna to the
Son of David," and Jesus was pleased with
their song. So now, and at all times, though
you do not see Him, the Lord Jesus is " in
His holy temple," and I think I see Him
smile with gladness as He listens to your
sweet voices shouting His praise.

1. Children should sing Hosanna to
Christ, *because He is so lovely and so glorious.*
Read His life in the gospel, and see what a

beautiful life it was. He was always going about and doing good, always gentle and kind, even to those who hated Him, and His great heart was brim-full of love for everybody. Read about His going to the throne in Heaven, where He is King over all His worlds, and can you help *praising* so wonderful a Being?

2. And think what He has *done for you.* Why, He has died that you might live forever in glory—has laid down His life for His precious lambs, to save their souls from being torn and devoured by Satan.

At a prayer-meeting in Brooklyn a little while ago, there was heard a low, sobbing voice of a poor little Irish 'girl, saying over and over again these three words, " Jesus, save me," " Jesus, save me." These were all the words that she knew how to use ; but she felt that she was a poor, lost sinner, and that Christ had died to save her, and so she kept repeating her little prayer till Jesus answered it, and her heart was made very happy. Oh, we need not offer long prayers to bring down the answer. I am sure that any child here can say those three words, and if you will say them, *feeling* every word, and wishing with all your heart to be saved, you may be just as happy as she was. And when she felt that Christ had saved her, and made her God's own child, she sang a new song of praise to His name. Well, this little girl wanted to show her Sunday-school teacher how thankful she was to her for her kind instructions. But what could she give? She was very poor, and had not even one cent, and could buy nothing. Presently she had a happy thought · she took a strip of canvas and worked in it the three words of her first prayer, " *Jesus save me*," and then cut off a piece of her bonnet string, and sewed it on that, and gave it to her teacher for a book-mark. At another prayer-meeting in Brooklyn, a gentleman told this story, and all at once nine persons rose up, and asked them to pray that the same Jesus might save them; and some of them, before they went home that night, began to sing of the love of Christ that had saved them too, and given them a hope of glory. Oh, how can we help praising such a loving Saviour, who has given *Himself* for us?

Let me tell you of another child, who lay on a bed of sickness. She had that awful disease that has laid so many little bodies in the grave, *Diptheria.* Her mother told her that she must die, and asked her whether she was ready to meet her God. The suffering girl looked tenderly at her mother, and tried to speak, but could not; and then she made a motion with her hand, as if she would like to write. They handed her a pencil and paper. Feebly the pale fingers grasped the pencil, and wrote one word, "*unworthy,*" and then she closed her eyes and her head fell back upon the pillow. But presently a heavenly smile broke over her face, and she took the pencil again and wrote, "*Jesus Christ*": and when she had finished the last letter, her hand dropped, and her soul went to be with her Lord and Saviour—went to sing "Hosanna to the Son of David," with the blessed angels in glory. Now, like her, we are all "*un worthy*," but *Jesus* will save us as He did her, if we give our hearts to Him. Ought we not, then, to *praise Him?*

3. Another reason why children should praise Jesus is, because *this is the way to make this world like heaven, and to become ourselves like the blessed angels.*

Do you not sometimes wish you could hear the angels singing, so as to know whether their songs are anything like ours? I hope we may all hear them and sing with them by-and-by; but I can tell you now one of their songs, for the prophet John once heard it, and he has written it down

for us in the Book of Revelation. Suppose
that we could all be lifted to the *upper*
" gate of heaven," and listen for a moment
to what is going on inside. We should
hear music sweeter than we ever dreamed
of before. But the *words* would not be
strange to us. They would be very much
like those of the children in the temple—
" Hosanna to the son of David!"—for
John tells us that they sing the praises of
God and of *the Lamb*—that is of Jesus—
and shout, "Worthy is the Lamb that was
slain!"

Do you not see, then, that when we sing
about Jesus we are doing just what the
angels do, and what all who have gone
from this world to heaven are now doing,
and what *we* shall do if we ever get to that
holy, happy place? And if you do not love
to sing and pray to Jesus *now*, do you think
you can be happy in that world where
every one is loving and praising Him?

17

You have often sung those beautiful words, "I want to be an angel." Do you want to be one, really? Then try to love, and sing, and serve the Saviour like an angel, (and you need not wait till you get to heaven to do that,) and you will find in it a sweet joy and peace that the world can never give you.

A gentleman once said to a young lady, who was the sweetest singer in the choir, "*What will you do with that voice in eternity?*" The more the young lady thought of the solemn question, the more she felt that her voice was given her to praise the Saviour with, and that this was the best use she could make of it here; and so she gave Him all her heart, and voice, and strength to praise and serve Him.

And oh, your voice, dear child, what will you do with it *in eternity*, if you do not *now* begin to obey and serve the Lord Jesus? He now asks you for that voice, that He may tune it to the heavenly anthems. He asks you for that *heart*, that He may attune it to heavenly pleasures. Oh, give yourselves up to Him, and be happy!

There are many, many children in the great house of God on high, singing to-day, Hosanna to the Son of David. But though they sing ever so sweetly, yet there are *other voices* which Jesus wants to hear. The great choir of heaven is not yet filled up. Its music is not yet strong and loud enough, and there are many harps of gold all ready for those who will take them. Oh, give your hearts to Jesus, and then you will be so happy that you can no more help singing than the birds can help it. And you know *the morning* is the time when the birds sing the most sweetly. So the morning of your life is the time for you to praise the Lord Jesus. And do not think that you must praise Him with your *voice* only. Show how much you love Him by *obeying* Him in your lives; and let everything you do and say be like the different parts of one great, long "Hosanna to the the Son of David!" Then, when death comes, although his cold hand upon your lips will stop every other song, it cannot stop your praises to the dear Redeemer, but you shall

> "With the angels stand,
> A crown upon your forehead, a harp within your
>   hand,
> And right before your Saviour, so glorious and so
>   bright,
> You'll wake the sweetest music, and praise Him
>   day and night."

IX.

The Crown and Kingdom Won.

" Little travellers, Zion-ward,
　　Each one entering into rest,
　In the kingdom of your Lord,
　　In the mansions of the blest—
　There, to welcome, Jesus waits,
　　Gives the crowns His followers win.
　Lift your heads, ye golden gates,
　　Let the little travellers in.

" All our earthly journey past,
　　Every tear and pain gone by,
　Here together met at last
　　At the portals of the sky:
　Each the welcome, ' COME,' awaits,
　　Conquerors over death and sin:
　Lift your heads, ye golden gates,
　　Let the little travellers in !"

17*　　　　　　　　　　(197)

The Crown and Kingdom Won.

"And the streets of the city shall be full of boys and girls, playing in the streets thereof."—ZECHARIAH viii. 5.

WHAT is more pleasant than to see children playing happily together about their quiet homes without any fear of being harmed! How sad and dreary any place would be if, when we walked through the streets, or looked into the houses or yards, we should hear no glad shouts of boys or girls at play! Now, if you had been in the city of Jerusalem when the prophet Zechariah wrote these words, you would have seen a very gloomy place. You would have seen a great many empty houses, with their walls tumbling to the ground, and large heaps of ashes and cinders where the best part of the city had

(199)

been ; and you would have seen only a very
few children there ; and they would have
run away, frightened, at the face of a
stranger.

Why was this? Ah, the little Jewish
boys and girls whose houses were so silent
and dreary were, most of them, away off in
Babylon. Their parents had become very
wicked, and, as I have told you before, God
punished them by letting a great king carry
them away and make them servants in his
own country. But were the Jews never to
come back to their homes in Jerusalem?
Yes. for now they began to be very sorry
for their sins, and to give back their hearts
to God, and to pray to Him. And God
heard their prayers, and sent His prophet
to tell them that their city should be built
up again ; and, to show them how happy
and peaceful they then should be, He said
that the streets, which were now so lonely,
should yet be "*full of boys and girls, play-*

ing." And in a few years it all came to pass, just as God had said.

But it is about *another city* that I now wish to talk with you. The Apostle Paul speaks of " the *heavenly* Jerusalem," and the " Jerusalem which is *above ;*" and John, in the book of Revelation, calls Heaven the " *New* Jerusalem." I shall now try to tell you something about that holy, heavenly city, whose golden streets are " full of boys and girls," and about the way to get there.

I. And, first, how shall I describe to you that city? It is more beautiful than we can even *think* of. There are many splendid cities in this world, but none that are half as glorious as heaven. There are many happy homes all around us, but none that are half as happy as those mansions of our Father's house on high.

Let us now try to look in through the gates of that city, and see some of its glories. How can we do this? We look up into the blue sky, but, though we try ever so hard, we can see nothing beyond it. And when night comes on we watch the bright stars twinkling like silver crowns upon us, and wonder if some star, brighter than the rest, may not be the city where our crowns are waiting for us, but still we do not see Heaven. A child who was once looking with wonder upon the stars, asked if they were not holes in the floor of heaven, to let the glory through. Another, a little girl in Sweden, walking with her father one night, looked up to the starry skies and said. "Father, I have been thinking if the wrong side of heaven is so beautiful, *what must the right side be !*" And a poet has beautifully said,

> " Since o'er Thy *footstool* here below
> Such radiant gems are strewn,
> O ! what magnificence must glow,
> My God, about *Thy throne !*"

Yet, after all, we can see but a very small number of the stars with our eyes alone; and so men make what they call *telescopes*, and when we look through them we can see thousands and millions of stars a great way off, that we could not see before—yet even then we cannot see *heaven*. But God has given us something better than a telescope, and if we look through it we can see that "happy land" that is so "far, far away." I mean *the Bible*, which helps the eye of the soul to look beyond the stars, right into the holy city, and to see the kingdom and the crown that is prepared for those who love Jesus.

Let us look together through this clear, strong glass of heavenly truth, and what do we see? In the next to the last chapter of the Bible we see that heaven is a place where ' God shall wipe away all tears" from His people's eyes: where " there shall be no more death, neither sorrow nor cry-

ing, neither shall there be any more pain."
How glorious! No tears, no death, no
pain! O, "what must it be to be
there!"

But let us look again, and find out *what
makes it* such a happy place. "He that
overcometh shall inherit all things ," that
is, *all these* things. What does this mean?
Why, that every one who conquers sin and
Satan, and who is good and holy, and whose
sins have been washed away by the blood
of Jesus, shall go there. Heaven is happy
only because it is *holy*. It is nothing but
sin that causes all our tears and pains, and
sicknesses, and our death. Have you not
found out that you are never happy when
you do wrong? when you are angry, or en-
vious, or disobedient? This shows that no
place can be happy where sin is. If heaven
were an hundred times more beautiful than
it really is, no one with a wicked heart
could be happy there, for *holiness makes*

heaven, and sin makes hell. This is the reason why our wicked hearts must be changed for new and holy ones before we can go to that happy place.

But let us look once more at the holy city, for we cannot look at it too often. The prophet John says that an angel came and carried him away in spirit to a great and high mountain, and " showed him that great city, the holy Jerusalem, descending out of heaven from God, having the glory of God ; and her light was like unto a stone most precious." And it " had a wall great and high, and had twelve gates, and at the gates twelve angels." And a little further on he says, ' the twelve gates were twelve pearls ;" " and the street of the city was of pure gold ;" " and the city had no need of the sun, neither of the moon to shine in it, for the glory of the Lord did lighten it, and the Lamb is the light thereof."

What a beautiful place, all shining with

18

gold and gems! Would you not love to be there?

Let me tell you a story of a child who saw heaven in her dreams. "I dreamed," said little Ellen, "that I stood outside the gate of heaven, and looked in. The gate was all made of precious stones; but I could see through it. I could see the street, and it was all pure gold. I saw angels playing on large harps; and I heard such singing as I never heard on earth. They were all singing the same words; but I could not tell what they were. As I was looking, God spoke to me. He asked me if I had a new heart. I told him I did not know. He said, 'If you have not, you cannot come in here; but, if you will go back to earth, and pray for it, you shall have one, and I will send an angel and bring you up here.'

"So I went back to earth, and went into a closet; and, as I was praying, an angel

came and took me, and put me in one side
of his bosom, and dear sister Annie in the
other, and carried us up to heaven. You
don't know how sweetly we looked. We
were just like two little flowers tucked in
his bosom.

"When we came to the gate, an angel
opened it for us, and we went in. Before,
when I heard the music, I thought I never
could sing like that; but, the moment I
was in, I could sing as well as any of them.
Angels were all the while coming, bringing
little babies in their bosoms; and, the moment they were in, they would sing as loud
and as sweet as the rest. I saw my mother;
and she looked glorious and beautiful. She
was playing on a harp, and singing, oh! so
sweetly! Grandmother, too, was there;
and, oh! Annie, her wrinkles were all
gone; and she looked as young as you do;
and her face shone, and she was singing
too. I said, 'Grandmother, there was great

weeping when you left earth.' She said,
'Yes ; but I would not like to go back.' I
saw Jesus sitting on a throne, and angels
worshipping him ; and when I saw how
bright and glorious everything was, I
wished that I had never sinned."

Yes, dear children, I am sure that will
be the wish of all of us, if we ever get
there, that we had *never sinned.*

But this was only a dream, and the Bible
is better than all the dreams and visions men
have ever had. Read and study the Bible,
and you will find that the glories of heaven
are greater than any earthly eye has seen,
or ear has heard, or mind has thought of.
The fact is, they are so great that they cannot be told to us. If a bright angel were
to come down from heaven on purpose to
tell us about them, I believe that he would
tremble and stammer and hesitate, and
then say, as Paul did, after he had been
caught up to heaven, that the things which

he had seen there it was *not possible to utter*.

Now, may *children* go to that beautiful city? May *little feet* walk in those golden streets, and *little hands* play on the harps of heaven, and *little voices* sing with the angels " the song of Moses and the Lamb"?

II. Yes ; and I wish now to show you, in the second place, that, like the old Jerusalem, the *New* Jerusalem is "*full of boys and girls:*" that, in the words of the beautiful hymn,

> " Around the throne of God in heaven
>   *Thousands of children* stand ,
> Children whose sins are all forgiven,
>   A holy, happy band,
>   Singing, ' Glory be to God on High '"

Do you know that more than one-half of all the people who are born into this world die when they are very small? Perhaps

18*

some of you have lost a little brother or sister, a sweet, beautiful babe, whom you had
just learned ·to love very dearly when God
took it from you, and it was buried out of
your sight. You remember how you wept
when you saw the tiny hands folded so cold
and still, and the bright eyes closed, and
found that, although you called ever so
loudly, you could not make it hear. Yes, a
great many of us have followed these little
ones to the grave ; and now, all over the
world, sweet, lovely children are dying.

> " There is no flock, however watched and tended,
>   But one dead lamb is there."

Now, what becomes of these little ones
who have hardly begun to live before they
die ? We know where their *bodies* are, but
where are their *souls ?* I believe that our
Saviour answered the question, when he said,
" Suffer the little children to come unto me,
and forbid them not, for *of such is the king-*

dom of heaven." Jesus, like a good Shepherd, takes up these little lambs in His arms, and carries them in His bosom safe to His heavenly fold ; and so

> " Millions of *infant souls* compose
> The family above."

I have told you of a little girl's dream of heaven. Once there was a minister, Mr. Finley, who had something like a vision of the Holy City, and of the little children there. He was very sick ; and when his friends were weeping about his bed, and waiting to see him die, he thought he saw an angel come to him, and take him on his wings to heaven. The great high gates rolled back upon their golden hinges, and as he entered he saw the most beautiful objects. Before him was the " pure river of water of life, clear as chrystal," and upon each side of the river beautiful trees, all covered with fruits and flowers. Bright angels were floating in the air, and flying back and forth from this world. But he said that the most lovely thing that he saw there was *a little child*. "There was nothing with which the blessed babe could be compared. Its wings were long and beautiful, and tinged with all the colors of the rainbow. Its dress seemed to be of the whitest silk, covered with the softest white down. Its face was all radiant with glory ; its very smile," said he, "now plays around my heart. I gazed and gazed with wonder upon this heavenly child."

At length he said, "If I have to return to the earth, I should love to take this child with me, and show it to the weeping mothers of the earth. I think when they see it they will never shed another tear over their children when they die." Then he tried to take it in his arms, but it flew from him to one of the topmost boughs of the Tree of Life, and then sweetly looked on him, and began singing, "To Him that hath loved me, and washed me from my sins in His own blood, to Him be glory, both now and forever. Amen."

When the -good man awoke from this dream he clasped his hands for joy, and sprang from his bed, and could not stop praising God. Now, whether he saw a *real* angel-child or not, of this we may be sure, the little ones in glory are even more beautiful and happy than he could describe, or than any of us can know until we see them there.

But besides these little babes of Jesus, as we may call them, who die before they can speak the name of Christ, there are very many *older* boys and girls who have gone up to the shining streets of the New Jerusalem. For, Christ loves all the children who love Him. He died just as much for them as for the parents: and when He says, " They that seek me early shall find me," it is just as if He threw the pearly gates wide open to all of the young who will enter them. I cannot

begin to tell you how many have loved and
served the Saviour, and then in childhood
or youth have been caught up·by the angels
to glory. Some of your friends and play-
mates, perhaps, are there : and great multi-,
tudes from the Sabbath-schools, and churches,
and blessed Christian homes all over the wide
world. O, if we could see them now with
their bright, happy faces, each wearing his
golden crown, and singing more sweetly than
they ever sung upon earth—I am sure we
should want to be with them, and be happy too!

A teacher once taught her little class the
verse, " Suffer little children to come unto
me, and forbid them not, for of such is the
kingdom of heaven." That afternoon, after
school was dismissed, a little boy whose name
was Willie, (and whose loving heart and
smiling face made him a little sunbeam where-
ever he went,) came softly back and put his
arms around his teacher's neck and kissed
her, saying, in his lisping way

"I love oo, tecer."

"What is love, Willie," she asked.

He thought a moment, and then said, "Its what makes us dood to folks." Presently he said, "Tecer, who is Kwist that b'est 'ittle children?"

Before the teacher could answer, she was called away, and little Willie went home. The next day he did not come to school, and the teacher went to his house to see if he was sick. On the way there she met his sister, who said to her,

"Oh! teacher, won't you come right down to our house; Willie is so sick, and don't know any of us."

In a few minutes she stood by his bedside. He was tossing about with pain, but all the time kept saying softly, "Who is Kwist that b'est 'ittle children?" The teacher sat down by his side, and told him the sweet story of the cross, but Willie's mind was as sick as his body, and he could not understand her.

And still he asked earnestly, "Pleath tell me who is Kwist that b'est 'ittle children."

" Will you pray for us?" asked the father. Then the teacher knelt and prayed that God would spare the darling boy, or if not, that He would comfort the hearts of his parents.

When they arose from their knees the little form writhed in agony. Then he lay still with closed eyes and clasped hands. Then, in about an hour, there was another convulsion longer and harder than the last. When it was over he opened his eyes, and his pale lips parted, and he said with a strange, pleading earnestness, as if his whole soul was speaking,

" Pleath tell me who is Kwist that b'est 'ittle children ; oh, *pleath* tell me!"

" Pray for him, *for him*," sobbed the father. And the teacher did pray, as she had never prayed before, that Christ would show Himself to the dying child.

God heard that prayer ; for soon a happy

look passed over• Willie's face. He lifted his head, and stretched out his small, white hands towards heaven, and said,

" *There is Kwist that b'est 'ittle children. I coming—I coming!*" and so little Willie's spirit went to be with Christ, whom he had sought so earnestly, and there was one more angel-child in glory.

And heaven is all the time filling up with just such blessed, happy children. But that city is not yet full. As Jesus says in the parable, " *Yet there is room;*" room for all, crowns and harps for all, and a Saviour's loving smile for all who will now love and obey Him.

III. But I must say a few words about *the way to get to the Holy City.*

We cannot see the way to heaven as we see the way to the church and Sabbath-school—that is, with these bodily eyes—for, as Paul says, " *We walk by faith,* not by

19

sight." But we can see that way with the *eye of the soul*, by believing and obeying what God has told us, and by taking Christ at His word when he says, "Him that cometh unto me I will in no wise cast out;" and, "Believe on the Lord Jesus Christ and thou shalt be saved."

What is it to believe? I will tell you.

In the highlands of Scotland there is a narrow place only twenty feet wide and two hundred feet deep, the walls on each side running straight down, but with here and there a little spot or crevice where grow many beautiful flowers. A gentleman once offered a little boy a handsome present if he would consent to be let down into that deep place by a rope, and gather a basket full of the flowers for him. The boy looked wishfully at the money, for his parents were poor but when he looked down into the terrible place where he was to go, he was afraid. But presently his heart grew strong, and his eyes sparkled, and he said, " I will go *if my father holds the rope.*" Then his father tied the rope around him, and lowered him down, and when he had filled his basket, lifted him safely to the top again. Why was he not afraid? Because he had *faith* in the strength of his father's arm, and in the love of his father's heart, that would not let him perish.

So God wants you to have faith in Him, and in Jesus Christ His Son. Christ is like a rope let down from heaven to keep you from perishing. Let your hearts cling to Jesus, just as the hands of the little boy clung to his rope; and you may know that it will not break, for your heavenly Father holds it, but will lift you up to where the Father is, and where there are so many happy, angel children who have gone the same way before you.

Let a dying girl preach to you about Jesus, and how to come to Him and be saved in heaven. She was a Sunday scholar in Ireland, about thirteen years old. She was very weak, but as she lay on her dying bed, struggling for breath, her face, like Stephen's, shone "like the face of an angel," so full was she of heavenly joy. She was almost too feeble to speak ; but she had six or eight of her little friends by her bedside, and was *preaching Christ* to them.

"Oh Jane dear," she would say, "Oh Annie, come to Jesus! come to Him! He'll not put you away! O give him your heart : give Him *all* your heart, for I know He will not take half of your heart! Give Him all your heart, and He'll take away all your sins, and make you as happy as He has made me. *Pray to Him* for His Holy Spirit, and He will hear you. But remember, *trust Him*, have faith in Him, else He will not hear you. I used to pray to Him before I had not faith in Him, and he did not hear me. Oh," she exclaimed, "that all the children in Belfast would come to Jesus.

He has room for them all—He would save them all!"

Thus preached that dying girl, and I do not know that any one could better point out the way to be saved than she did.

Now dear children, will you not give your hearts to Jesus, that he may wash them in His blood from all their sins, and fit them for the crowns and kingdom in glory?

CPSIA information can be obtained
at www.ICGtesting.com
Printed in the USA
BVHW041110240119
538585BV00016B/378/P